*Creative Cooking*

Books by Nicholas Roosevelt:

CREATIVE COOKING
A FRONT ROW SEAT
A NEW BIRTH OF FREEDOM
THE TOWNSEND PLAN
AMERICA AND ENGLAND?
THE RESTLESS PACIFIC
THE PHILIPPINES: A TREASURE AND A PROBLEM

Creative Cooking

by NICHOLAS ROOSEVELT

Introduction by DIONE LUCAS

Harper & Brothers Publishers New York

CREATIVE COOKING
Copyright © 1956 by Nicholas Roosevelt
Printed in the United States of America
All rights in this book are reserved.
No part of the book may be used or reproduced in any manner whatsoever without written permission except in the case of brief quotations embodied in critical articles and reviews. For information address Harper & Brothers 49 East 33rd Street, New York 16, N. Y.

FIRST EDITION

H-F

Library of Congress catalog card number: 56-8759

*To my fellow members
of the American Garlic Society*

ACKNOWLEDGMENTS

Four ladies—good cooks, all of them—played a large part in the making of this book: my wife, who not only taught me much about cooking good food but appraised my culinary adventures with discrimination and patience even when I used every pot and tool in the kitchen; my sister-in-law, Katherine Dillon Gates, who prodded me into writing this book, helped outline it and made invaluable suggestions in redrafting it; Melissa Blake Levitzky, who uncomplainingly copied and recopied every page, helped make the index and suggested wise modifications of the text; and Betty Tolerton, who carefully edited and proofread the manuscript and galleys. To them I owe my thanks.

TABLE

OF CONTENTS

FOREWORD   xiii

INTRODUCTION   xvii

1. GENERAL PRINCIPLES   1

   Enjoy good eating. Variety is fundamental. Seasoning: the secret of good food. Recipes are not rigid. Be bold: take a chance. Imagination: you can develop it. Planning is essential. Timing will make cooking—and living—easier. Appearances are part of civilized eating. Serve hot things hot. Good ingredients facilitate good cooking. Master the elements of cooking processes. Taste as you go.

2. THINGS TO AVOID   13

   Overseasoning. Killing natural flavors with strong sauces. Overcooking. Using too much fat. Using high heat—with exceptions. Overfrying garlic. Melting cheese fast. Expecting canned soup to replace soup stock. Considering canned food as "ready to serve."

3. THE ART OF SEASONING   21

Do not overdo. You are the judge. Classification of seasonings. Natural seasonings. Herbs, their use and abuse. Dried herbs. Spices. Bottled seasonings. Other seasonings. Wine in cooking.

4. SOME SAUCE SECRETS   37

Extractive sauces. Component sauces. *Roux*, the basis of most sauces. The versatile white sauce. Some much-used sauces. Independent sauces. To thicken a sauce. Uncooked sauces. Mayonnaise. Vinaigrette. The creamed butters. The importance of sauce making.

5. THE CHALLENGE OF THE EGG   52

Fried eggs. Scrambled eggs. Poached eggs. The art of the omelet. The easy soufflé. Shirred eggs. Eggs Static.

6. BEAUTIFUL SOUP   67

Meat stocks. Chicken stock. The uses of stock. Thick soups. Vegetable soups. Chowders. Canned soups. Dried soups. Accompaniments for soups. Last words on soups.

7. FISH—FINE FARE   84

Canned fish. Frozen fish. Fresh fish. Smoked fish. Shellfish. Crustaceans.

Table of Contents

8. **SIX HUNDRED MILLION CHICKENS** — 99

    Why fried? Classes of chickens. Broilers, grilled and broiled. Baking broilers or fryers. Chickens in casseroles. Roast chicken. The importance of stuffing. Chicken leftovers. Chicken stock. Chicken sold in pieces. Turkeys now are small. Ducks, domestic and wild. Squabs—for big money.

9. **MANY MEN'S MEAT** — 118

    Cooking for few. Kinds of meat. Grilling over charcoal. Broiling by gas or electricity. Roasting means baking. Pan frying. Stews by any other name. The useful casserole. Meat loaves. Meat reserves.

10. **VARIED VEGETABLES** — 135

    Fresh and frozen vegetables. Delicate vegetables. Coarse vegetables. Mild vegetables. Pepping up potatoes. Yams and sweets. Canned vegetables. Dried legumes.

11. **SOME SO-CALLED STARCHES** — 152

    The useful pastas. Pastas should not be overcooked. Seasoning the pastas. Cheese is indispensable. Risottos. Pilaffs. Curries. Wild rice.

12. **SALAD ESSENTIALS** — 161

    Basic salad. Dressing the salad. Variants of French dressing. Mayonnaise. Salads as meals. The indispensable garlic.

13. **THE END OF A PERFECT MEAL** — 170

    The merits of fruits. Dried fruits. Three pound-adders. In praise of cheese. Eat, but don't run. Coffee for cowboys—and kings.

14. **Wine and Strong Drink** — 179

The classification of wines. Sherry as an appetizer. Dessert wines. Table wines. Good American vineyards. Imported wines. The care and serving of wines. Wines for celebrations. Strong drinks. The serving of liqueurs.

15. **Plan to Plan** — 192

Three kinds of planning. Long-range planning. Planning ahead: (1) counting mouths; (2) use fresh foods first; (3) contrasts in color; (4) hot food deserves hot plates; (5) the mechanics of serving; (6) cutting down last-minute chores; (7) changing menus in mid-air. Planning for each dish. Preparation often slow.

16. **Odds and Ends** — 203

Leftovers. Substitutes. Food friends. Some kitchen gadgets. A place for seasonings. Deep freezing not eternal.

17. **The Care and Feeding of Guests** — 210

Guests present problems. Hints on mechanics. Keep them moving. The unavoidable time lag. The role of snacks. Not "what" but "how." Who sits where. Silence can be golden. The compleat guest room. Helping the hostess. "Good night, sweet prince."

18. **Sex in the Kitchen** — 221

A Postscript on Cookbooks — 225

INDEX — 227

FOREWORD

Anyone who writes a cookbook should expect to be asked: "What do you know about cooking?"

I answer:

My earliest recollection of enjoying food goes back to camping trips with former President Theodore Roosevelt in my boyhood, when he fried steaks and chickens in bacon grease. His children and young cousins were sure no better food existed anywhere. More mature judgment suggests that T.R. was a better President than cook.

In the half century that has passed since then work and play have taken me to Europe, the Far East, Latin America and many parts of the United States. Always I have been interested in what I had to eat. From the chef of the American Legation in Budapest, where I served as United States Minister in the early 1930's, I acquired an understanding of the difference between excellent and ordinary food. He had studied cooking in Paris and was one of the best chefs in Hungary, where good food was relished. Each morning he and I planned the next day's meals—often for as many as twenty or thirty guests. As he loved postprandial post-mortems, he would ask how a particular dish had been received by the guests the day before and tell me what went into its making. He never tired of analyzing dishes, and of discussing ways to change or improve them. In fact, the keenness of his interest in what he cooked was one of the reasons why he was so competent, and the sharpness of his questions made me conscious of subtleties of taste of which I might otherwise have remained unaware.

So much for my culinary background. My only formal schooling in cookery was an all too brief period as a pupil of Mrs. Dione Lucas, who has been gracious enough to write the introduction to this book, and who, when I studied under her, was head of the Cordon Bleu School of Cooking in New York. Even more valuable than the excellent recipes which she gave us were the many practical hints about the details of cooking, and the chance to watch an expert in action.

Foreword

That was before my wife and I moved to California ten years ago. Since then, of the last 10,000 meals which I have eaten I have had a part in the preparation of about 9,000. I have grilled at least 1,500 chickens and 750 steaks, and made 1,200 omelets and countless sauces, soups and casseroles. In the doing I learned much.

This book has been written in the hope that our experience will hearten others who enjoy good food and who face the twofold problem of preparing it without outside help and without spending all day in the kitchen. Emphasis throughout is on the "how" and the "good," rather than on recipes. Good cooking, as Mrs. Lucas has said, is an art, and no art can be learned by slavishly following rigid rules. Creativeness implies individuality and initiative. Creative cooking is particularly rewarding in that it can make life pleasanter for artist, family and friends.

INTRODUCTION

by Dione Lucas

In this book Nicholas Roosevelt has clarified the fundamentals of cooking for the beginner, and has given helpful reminders to the more experienced. *Creative Cooking* is just what the title indicates. The usual recipes have been eliminated, but the housewife or cook with a little imagination will need few recipes after absorbing the contents of this gratifying volume. It covers completely just about everything pertaining to food. He discusses the origin, growing, planning, buying, preparing, cooking, serving, eating and even the digestion of food. He tells you about pots, serving dishes, and all kinds of cooking and kitchen equipment. He even tells you how to plan a workable kitchen, and gives the hostess some hints on how to appear as cool as a cucumber when greeting her guests just after pulling her head out of a hot oven. He tells you how to enjoy good eating and how to keep your family or guests happy by serving a variety of food and using the best of ingredients—not necessarily the most expensive. He discusses last-minute cooking for the hostess, and what to do with leftovers. With the information and hints he gives you so profusely you will have courage to be bold and venturesome and will find great joy in your culinary creations.

Society at last is elevating cookery to its proper place among the creative arts. Eating should be a most important and pleasureful pastime, and yet so often we fail to give the preparation of food the thought and time it deserves. The erroneous opinion that cooking is only a necessary chore to be disposed of as quickly as possible, or to be assigned to domestic help, is vanishing and people are discovering new horizons in the culinary world.

With the lack of domestic help in this country more housewives are doing their own cooking and the focal point of the family is back in the kitchen—the warmest, savoriest and friendliest of rooms. When a professional cook is employed by a family the kitchen usually

Introduction

becomes out of bounds for the children, and they are deprived not only of its kindly atmosphere but of an opportunity to learn some of the fundamentals of preparing the family repast. There are some things we can only learn properly by doing, or by watching the performance of one with experience. I have always regretted that so many of the young women who attended my cooking classes had a wealth of education in the arts and sciences but had had no basic cooking courses in school, or experience in their own kitchens.

In my own case I felt a strong urge at an early age to cook. I was brought up in a family of artists and musicians and given cello lessons, and although my love of music was important it was secondary to my interest in cooking. Because my intelligent mother considered cooking one of the creative arts I was encouraged to pursue my first love, and it has been a very rewarding and satisfying creative experience. No artist could have a more appreciative public than can a cook capable of producing culinary masterpieces, and what is more fulfilling than applause from your family? I have found working for these goals most inspiring.

No other period in history can boast of the delicacies our farmers and food producers have supplied us with in such abundance through their inventiveness and diligence. Nowhere in the world is food as plentiful as in the United States. By air freight and modern refrigeration we are supplied with fresh fruit and vegetables out of season—an unheard-of luxury in the past. The manufacturers offer us time- and energy-saving kitchen equipment, with lovely pots that can be used for cooking on top of the stove and in the oven, and yet are so attractive that they can be placed on the table as serving dishes. All of these contributions are helping to enliven and inspire the culinary interests not only of contemporary women but of our men.

Creative Cooking is a book of valuable suggestions that only years of experience, love of good food, and appreciation of the culinary art could inspire. The chapter on sauces is equal to a cookbook within itself, giving you basic recipes for every sauce imaginable, and then telling you how to enhance them. Sauces are the added touch or embellishment that can change a food from a dull nourishment to a dish for the gods, can change the texture of dry stringy meat to juicy lusciousness—or, if not done with care and knowledge, can be disastrous.

The same is true of seasoning, which is the personal touch that can make a dish delectable or ruin it, and with differences in ingredients it is impossible always to follow a recipe exactly and have it come out just

Introduction xxi

right. All of this Mr. Roosevelt also abundantly makes clear.

There are chapters on eggs, soups, poultry, fish, meats, starches, vegetables, salads and desserts—all enlightening—as well as a most helpful and illuminating chapter on herbs and other flavorings. The book is sincere and charming, with touches of humor and historical data that make it delightful reading. I think you will agree with me that it is ironical that a book of this caliber has finally been written by a man. In retrospect I am not surprised that I have always regarded Nicholas Roosevelt as the most talented cuisinier I ever taught.

# GENERAL 1
PRINCIPLES

ENJOY GOOD EATING

The enjoyment of good food is a mark of civilized living. It is not to be confused with gluttony. Nor is it something only the rich can afford. Rather does it mean making of a necessary daily function—the ingestion of food—something which is anticipated eagerly, savored with relish, and looked back upon with satisfaction. Good food should be eaten in pleasant surroundings, in a friendly and unhurried atmosphere, and should be the subject of frank and interested conversation. If a dish has been well made, the cook should be praised. Perhaps in time hidebound Americans will pay tribute to good cooking in the French manner of sopping up the last drop of gravy with a bit of bread.

All of which boils down to the simple fact that if you like good food you will learn to cook well. If you don't care, don't cook.

VARIETY IS FUNDAMENTAL

If there is any single rule which a would-be cook should heed, it is the importance of variety. The same dish should never be served in the same form with the same seasoning two meals, or even two days, in succession. The wife who takes her husband's avowed preference for fried eggs for breakfast literally, and serves them day after day, is more likely to end up in a divorce court than is one who, if she feels obliged to fry his eggs, adds a bit of subtle seasoning of a different sort each day. But of this, more anon. The way to the heart may be through the stomach. But the way to the stomach surely is through ingenuity in varying the flavor of dishes which may be made of the same basic ingredients.

SEASONING: THE SECRET OF GOOD FOOD

The secret of seasoning is subtlety. Never overdo. Too much of anything can spoil the best dish.

General Principles

Strong flavors clash. Certain foods, if fresh and of good quality, have such delicate flavors by themselves that they should be eaten with nothing but a minimum of salt, and perhaps a dash of butter. This is true of vegetables such as peas and young beans. It is true of many types of fish, and of good broiling chickens and beef for grilling or roasting. Give them a chance.

RECIPES ARE NOT RIGID

With a few exceptions, most of which have to do with baking and the making of breadstuffs, recipes are not inflexible rules. They are merely suggestions. Try a new recipe which appeals to you just "as is"—the first time. Thereafter vary it. Experiment. Not only is this part of the fun of cooking, but it is the way good dishes have come into being. What the cookbook directs is less important than how you and your family or friends like the dishes you have prepared. Anyone can make edible mashed potatoes by following one of numerous standard recipes. But the adventurous cook who adds fresh herbs, or other kind of seasoning, is likely to turn out a dish which will be hailed with enthusiasm never accorded to conventional mashed potatoes. Consider recipes as general guides—but don't be the slave of a cookbook.

BE BOLD: TAKE A CHANCE

The late Marshal Foch of France was fond of repeating the old French aphorism: *"De l'audace! Toujours de l'audace!"* He used it in terms of military strategy. The principle applies also to culinary strategy. Be courageous. Don't be satisfied with copying a dish which you liked at a friend's house. Try to improve it. Incidentally, don't forget that there are people so low that they have been known to give a friend a recipe, deliberately omitting an important ingredient, so that the dish would be a flop.

By the same token, there is a solid—some call it smug—satisfaction in turning out your own edition of a friend's recipe which, thanks to your ingenuity and audacity, is better than the original. Next time ask her over to try it. You'll enjoy it, even if she doesn't.

IMAGINATION: YOU CAN DEVELOP IT

Imagination in cooking consists in projecting your sense of taste into the future of the dish you are contemplating or preparing, and remembering past flavors that you liked. If, for example, you find a soup too bland, and recall that you once improved a similar brew by adding lemon juice, try, instead, adding a few drops

General Principles

of good vinegar, or the juice of a fresh lime. If a small quantity of something is left over, try to think what might be added to it. The more you experiment, the more you will develop new and interesting flavors and food combinations, and the greater will be your confidence in your own imaginative powers. Each time you repeat a recipe which you already like, think how it would taste if you added a little of this or that, or omitted some prescribed ingredient. Take a chance. You may produce something rather bad. But you may also become a kitchen Columbus.

PLANNING IS ESSENTIAL

The object of good cooking is to make dishes which you and your family and guests will enjoy. Incidentally, meals can—and should—furnish a varied diet. Few doctors and nutritionists are agreed as to what constitutes a balanced diet, but if you have a variety of articles in the course of a day or a week the chances are that your system will absorb what it needs. If you are on a special regime, on your own or a doctor's advice, follow it at least until a new food fad lures you, or your doctor orders a change. The chances are it won't hurt you—always provided your food intake includes plenty of fresh fruits and vegetables, fresh milk, at least small quantities of meat or poultry, and, perhaps, some bread and cheese. If you like yoghurt, molasses, wheat germ, or yeast, give them a try. But do not despair if you fail to slough off the years and get rid of that tired feeling. Nature has a way of creeping up on us. Most Americans suffer not so much from food deficiencies as from overeating.

Wise planning also has an eye to follow-ups—to the planned use of remnants, so as to be able to cut down time in preparing a meal or two during succeeding days. In our household we plan meals for a week at a time, and change these plans at the drop of a hat—and on the arrival of unexpected guests.

TIMING WILL MAKE COOKING—AND LIVING—EASIER

It is helpful to figure out in advance how long it will take to prepare a meal. Certain preparations can be made hours before—some even the day before. Others MUST be made long in advance—especially if meat is to be marinated before cooking. Furthermore, it is wise except when living in the tropical summer climate of New York, Washington, Chicago, St. Louis and points south to take meat out of the refrigerator well in advance of the time it is to be cooked. The larger and colder the meat, the earlier it should be brought out.

Some dishes demand last-minute cooking or finishing. Otherwise they may be ruined. This is true of most fresh fish, of all omelets and of quick-cooking meats like liver. Soufflés and popovers also MUST be eaten the instant they are ready, even though these do not require attention from the cook after they have been put in the oven. Accordingly, in making your time schedule, allow for late arrivals, slow drinkers and other obstacles to good eating, and be sure your dish will not be ready until you and your guests are seated. If you have not trained your husband to do the last-minute necessaries in the kitchen, make him act as receptionist. If drinks are to be served, he'll find this easy and congenial.

APPEARANCES ARE PART OF CIVILIZED EATING

To the Apostle John is attributed the saying: "Judge not according to the appearance." His reference was to the tables of the law. Wise hostesses and good cooks do just the opposite when it comes to setting a table for a meal. In few of the civilized activities of gracious living are appearances more important. Not only should the table be in a pleasant location in the house, but it should always be spotlessly clean and arranged with an eye to color and appearance, no matter how simple or brief the meal, and how slim the family purse. Furthermore, it is essential that food be nicely presented, and attractively arranged on a serving dish. So many kinds of cooking dishes have been designed in recent years which look well as serving dishes that it is often possible to avoid transferring food from a hot pan to what is too often a cold platter. There can and should be something festive about every meal. It marks a break in the routine of work or play, and an agreeable occasion for bringing together family and friends. The traditional conduct of the exploring Englishman in darkest Africa always sitting down to his dinner in the jungle in a tuxedo has ceased being practical in these United States—if it ever was. But its equivalent—coming to a meal in something fresh and pleasant looking, after removing as much as possible of the day's grime—still has a part in civilized living.

SERVE HOT THINGS HOT

Many cold meals that have been planned to be eaten cold are excellent. But hot dishes served lukewarm and eaten off cold plates are an insult to the eaters

General Principles

and unfair to the cook. It is not necessary, in order to avoid the serving of partly chilled hot dishes, to follow the English custom of sitting down to a meal at the precise minute of the appointed hour even though some of the guests have not arrived. If you don't have a warming oven or some sort of dish warmer, you can devise ways of keeping dishes and plates hot until serving time. Should you be indifferent to this detail of making meals attractive, attention to it will repay you for the simple reason that you will be presenting your culinary efforts at their best.

GOOD INGREDIENTS FACILITATE GOOD COOKING

This means primarily that foods should be fresh. It doesn't mean that they need be costly. Few vegetables out of season are worth buying. Even vegetables in season are poor buys if they have been picked too long, or are too old. Excellent dishes can be made out of dried beans or rice provided they are well flavored. Many housewives make the mistake of trying to economize on such things as vinegar, wine for cooking, dried herbs and spices. And yet the amounts used even in cooking for six or eight people are so small that it is doubtful if they represent more than a cent or two per dish. The difference in flavor is notable between using a good imported cocktail sherry in the kitchen and a so-called cooking sherry. The latter is usually not a sherry and, being unfit to drink, is not worth using in cooking. Two or three tablespoons of sherry goes far in most dishes. A fifth holds fifty-two tablespoons. Even at three dollars a bottle—for which you can get an excellent imported sherry—this would come to six cents a tablespoon. Many people do not hesitate to serve at least two martinis per person before a meal. Each drink will have from two to four tablespoons of gin in it—and the bottle will cost about as much as a good sherry. Figure it out for yourself. Are you inviting guests for drinks or for a good meal? Incidentally, the most civilized eaters in the world, with the exception of the Scandinavians and Dutch, look on cocktails or hard liquor before a meal as a desecration. In behalf of the Swedes, Norwegians, Danes and Dutch it should be pointed out that their climate demands alcohol for internal heating and that the hard liquor with which they fortify themselves before meals is usually accompanied by delectable tidbits.

MASTER THE ELEMENTS OF COOKING PROCESSES

Your favorite cookbook can tell you most of the basic tricks of the trade. But here again, a few general principles may help.

General Principles 11

Pans

Cooking pans with heavy bottoms are preferable to light ones. They distribute and hold the heat better. It is hard to beat the glazed ironware imported from France, Belgium, Holland and the Scandinavian countries. Their initial cost is higher than most domestic pots and pans, but their life is longer and their usefulness greater.

Heat

Unless you are deep frying, or browning poultry or meat preparatory to putting it in a casserole, it is better to use too low rather than too high a heat. If you are boiling something, the less water used the better (so long as the pan doesn't dry out). Use only just enough heat to keep it boiling. With the exception of certain specialties like bread, cake and biscuits, you are likely to get better results in oven cooking if you keep the heat down—and cook slowly. Even in broiling it is well not to place the broiling pan too near the flame.

As in other fields the solution lies in experimenting. Start out by following the directions. Next time, reduce the heat and increase the time. The chances are you won't regret it.

TASTE AS YOU GO

If you are finicky you may hesitate to taste. Genteel cooks overcome other people's scruples by using one spoon to take a bit of the cooking food out of the pan, and deftly pouring it into another, which then goes into the cook's mouth. No less an authority than Dione Lucas, when we studied under her in New York years ago, took the highly practical view that unless you taste as you cook, you cannot be sure that everything is as it should be, culinarily speaking. The reason is simple—even if a recipe is being followed with special care, the precise flavor or condition of one or more of the ingredients may differ in different localities or on different occasions. This is notably true of certain seasonings, such as garlic, onions and fresh herbs. It is even truer of dried herbs, which frequently not only look like hay, but in fact have lost so much of their original flavor that it is hard to distinguish them from each other and from alfalfa.

THINGS 2
TO AVOID

Despite the wisdom in these pages, there is no short cut to good cooking. If merely following the recipes in a cookbook were a sure way to become a good cook the United States would be full of them, as cookbooks roll off the printing presses in astronomical figures daily. There is more to good cooking than meets the eye in the average cookbook. From which the moral may be deduced: the way to become a good cook is by trying, by experimenting and by inventing. It requires application—but it's worth it.

OVERSEASONING

As will be made clear in the chapter on seasoning, there is a difference between flavor, which is the natural taste of food such as chicken, onions, corn, tomatoes and other items, and seasoning, which is the process by which either a natural flavor is enhanced, or, if the food to be served is rather tasteless, it is made more enticing.

The nature of seasonings will be fully discussed below. Here we should note the adage attributed to the lawgiver of ancient Greece, Solon: "Nothing to excess." For twenty-five hundred years wise men—and poor cooks—have failed to follow this precept. The key word is "excess." There is such a thing as too little, as well as too much. If you use too little seasoning you risk serving dull fare. The goal is a happy mean, and the ideal is that no seasoning should be obtrusive.

KILLING NATURAL FLAVORS WITH STRONG SAUCES

Sauces were invented to make dull food attractive. In time many sauces acquired more importance than the foods which they were meant to disguise. Good sauces are not to be spurned. They are among the glories of the culinary art. But many foods, if fresh and rightly cooked with a minimum of seasoning, are so delectable that even the blandest of sauces tends to obscure the delicacy of the natural flavor. Wonderful dishes can be made in which chicken is a principal

Things To Avoid 15

component. But it is hard to improve upon the flavor of a young broiler grilled over charcoal, with nothing added but a bit of salt. Most fresh vegetables are at their best when cooked with no seasoning except salt—and very little of that. Melted butter improves vegetables and fish. A delicately flavored sauce like hollandaise is good with asparagus or artichokes or fresh broccoli. But when you embark on more ambitiously seasoned sauces, let them be the center of attention in that particular course—and combine them with foods which need embellishment.

OVERCOOKING

Meat cooked too long loses its flavor and becomes either tough or stringy. Cheese overcooked is death on dentures. Overcooked eggs are leathery and indigestible. Fish cooked too long becomes mushy and loses its distinctive taste. Cabbage boiled as New Englanders, Germans and the Irish have long loved to boil it—that is, in a vat, or at least a gigantic pot, until it is yellow and soggy—acquires a sulphurous taste. You can boil onions to a pulp—and spend a day getting the odor out of the curtains and rugs. Better to serve vegetables a little on the crisp side—with the notable exception of potatoes. Even these should be cooked just enough—which means only until you can spear them fairly easily with a fork. A cousin of ours (by marriage), who can afford—and has—a high-priced cook, takes special pride in cooking spinach herself. Her system: to put the spinach in the largest vessel in the kitchen and boil it for an hour. She always feels hurt when her guests, one after another, speak of having an allergy for spinach. There may be more than one way to kill a cow, but there certainly is no better way to kill a mess of spinach—and make it inedible.

USING TOO MUCH FAT

Greasy food gravitates toward the buttocks and the paunch. Furthermore, it is unappetizing. Of course, there are fats and fats, and there are dishes which cry for them—such as the pastas, and salads. But it is easier to spoil a dish by using too much rather than too little fat, either in its initial content, its cooking or its seasoning. Chinese food is noticeably free from fat. The French are careful to remove all excess fat from soups, sauces and other dishes. While this is partly for reasons of economy, it serves a gustatory purpose. Frying is responsible for much bad cooking. In the South, and in much of the West until a generation

Things To Avoid

ago, excessive partiality for fried foods led to almost universal "dyspepsia," which, in turn, brought about wide use of "pain killers," "tonics" and other patent medicines of which alcohol was a main ingredient. No wonder the enjoyment of poor health was widespread. Strong drink may be raging, as the author of the Book of Proverbs insists, but it is also a must for anyone condemned to a daily diet of lard-soaked "vittles."

USING HIGH HEAT—WITH EXCEPTIONS

Deep frying, which is the process by which food encased in a hopefully fatproof batter is plunged into several inches of hot fat, is one of the two chief exceptions to the rule of using low heat. The other is in certain oven-baked dishes such as popovers and Yorkshire pudding, and most breads and pastries. In this field it is well to follow directions. When, as sometimes happens, different cookbooks call for different temperatures for the same dish, we incline to use the lower, on the general principle that slower cooking nearly always means more thorough cooking.

OVERFRYING GARLIC

The number of kitchen crimes committed in the name of garlic—and obnoxious dishes produced by its misuse—is one reason why so many Americans, like nearly all north Europeans, take a dim view of this aid to good cooking. A way of judging whether the compiler of a cookbook knows much about cooking is to leaf through recipes which call for the use of garlic and onions. If the author or compiler directs that the two be put in hot fat at the same time, it is a safe bet that the recipe has not been tested, or that the author does not know good food when he or she eats it. Onions cook slowly even in hot fat. Garlic cooks rapidly even over a low heat. Put it in really hot fat, and it turns brown or black almost instantly, and leaves behind it a taste like gas escaping from the stove. But garlic cooked tenderly, slowly and reverently opens an endless vista of culinary delights. In its proper place we shall sing its praises and suggest how best to use it—and not to abuse it.

MELTING CHEESE FAST

Most cheeses are tricky when you try to cook them. If you toss them into very hot butter or something which is already boiling, they are likely to express their displeasure by refusing to amalgamate. Instead, they form either a tough solid mass or equally tough and rubbery strings. Thenceforth, they defy all efforts

Things To Avoid

to induce them to commingle with the dish in which you wished to use them. The secret lies in removing from the fire the liquid to which you wish to add grated or cut-up cheese, and letting it cool a bit. Then put in the cheese in not too large quantities at a time, stirring it vigorously, and bring it slowly to a boil. Occasionally even the most amenable cheese will get ornery when you try to cook it. If it does, admit defeat and devise a substitute for what you had planned.

EXPECTING CANNED SOUP TO REPLACE SOUP STOCK

Many recipes—especially those with a French background—call for the use of soup stock. Lovers of good food keep on hand at least a small quantity of soup stock. (See Chapter 6.) Its lack presents a problem. In time some of the makers of canned soup will put up a genuine soup stock. But the various canned consommés, bouillons and broths which we have tried have such a persistent and ineradicable flavor that they dominate anything into which they are put, and will override the delicacy of any seasoning you may have planned. Richardson and Robbins market a plain chicken broth with rice which is not too predominantly flavored. It is worth trying, if you do not make your own soup stock.

CONSIDERING CANNED FOOD AS "READY TO SERVE"

Technically speaking, the label on cans may be accurate. The contents may be heated and served "as is." But the fact that canned goods are made for mass consumption means that their flavor is reduced to the lowest common denominator. They can be great time-savers, and some of them can form the bases for good meals when combined ingeniously with other foods, and skillfully seasoned. A few of them, like canned tuna, sardines and anchovies, and like canned tomatoes and tomato extracts, are musts. Some of the soups are excellent. Many are useful as precooked ingredients for other dishes, but even the best can be improved by judicious seasoning.

THE ART 3
OF SEASONING

Roasting is a skill. But seasoning is an art. Like any art it demands of its devotees love, perseverance and imagination. Anyone can spoil good food by too much seasoning. To enhance and bring out delicate flavors, or make dull dishes delectable, calls for restraint, discrimination and experience.

DO NOT OVERDO

As already suggested, the old Greek saying, "nothing to excess," is the first principle of good seasoning. It is easy to add a little more of a particular ingredient which you think would improve the flavor. But it is hard to neutralize excess. This is why, in seasoning, it is wise to taste as you go, and add wtih discretion. Experiment, of course. But unless the dish is one in which a particular seasoning is to predominate, like a curry, or a tomato sauce for spaghetti, or a garlic sauce for eggplant, be sparing with strong and all-pervasive seasonings.

YOU ARE THE JUDGE

If after testing various seasonings you like some less than others, drop them, no matter how much your friends or your favorite cookbooks commend them. But give them a fair trial first—especially by reducing the quantity of seasoning called for.

CLASSIFICATION OF SEASONINGS

There are several types of seasonings. They may be considered under four heads: (a) natural seasonings; (b) dried and powdered herbs and spices; (c) bottled concentrates; and (d) miscellaneous seasonings.

Natural Seasonings

Besides salt, which though artificially prepared is a natural ingredient, the most useful seasonings of this class are to be found among the members of the onion tribe, and among fresh herbs.

The Art of Seasoning

Let us consider some of them:

ONIONS should be treated with respect. If the dish is to have a coarse, harsh flavor—and few good dishes should—then chop or grate strong onions and use them freely. If just a bit of onion flavor is called for, cut off the bottom of an onion, and with a teaspoon scoop out the juice which will exude from the cut end of the bulb. Some onions are strong, some mild. Your vegetable dealer should know.

Three other members of the onion family deserve special notice—chives, shallots and garlic.

CHIVES are often available in good markets, in little pots. They are easy to tend, and can be grown either from seed or by transplanting. They do wonders in many egg dishes, are fine in certain soups and can be useful in salads and other dishes. Cut them with kitchen scissors, or chop them if your prefer. A teaspoon of cut or chopped chives is likely to be plenty, unless you are cooking for many mouths. The flavor of chives is milder and less persistent than that of raw onion in any of its forms. Even if you live in an apartment, it is not hard to nourish a pot or two of chives. They are worth the care.

SHALLOTS, unfortunately, are scarce in the United States. Yet they are easy to grow if you have a bit of good soil in the sun. Many French recipes call for shallots—especially in sauces. Their delicacy of flavor has won them deserved acclaim. They are usually chopped or minced, and sautéed in a little butter even when they are to be used in a sauce. The tender young tops can be cut up and sprinkled on soup. If ever you come across shallots in the market, or if you have room to plant a row, they will repay you richly. Furthermore, once you start them, they are virtually perpetual, as they reproduce by dividing—or, to be strictly accurate, by putting out new bulblets from the parent set.

GARLIC, known to botanists as *Allium sativum*, and by scent to tourists in any of the Mediterranean countries, is the noblest member of the onion tribe. But garlic is not to be trifled with, even though strong stomachs can take it raw. The tradition persists in Mediterranean lands that it has curative and healing properties. If nutritionists ever turn their attention to it they may well find that this is so. For thousands of years raw garlic has been fed to sick children. Garlic lovers are usually healthy, although garlic haters snidely insist that you have to be healthy to stomach garlic—which statement not only is open to challenge on grounds of fact, but exposes the person who makes it to the charge of having a reactionary palate or closed taste buds. Garlic has always had its detractors—as has any truly good thing when used to excess. The Roman poet Horace was an alliophobe (garlic hater to you). Most northern Europeans, with the exception of the French, are prejudiced against garlic. Many not only don't recognize it when they see it, but are so ignorant of its true properties that they do not even know that it was just a touch of garlic which gave a particularly delicious flavor to a salad or other admired dish eaten in a French or Italian restaurant. This is an excellent example of blissful ignorance.

Take care in the feeding of garlic. Without garlic there can be little good cooking. But garlic should be used in minute quantities, and never served raw in bits or slices. One of the great inventions of modern gadgetry is the so-called garlic press, which is like a tiny potato squisher. With this you can extract a bit of the juice of garlic, or a few fine shreds—and remember that even a full drop of garlic juice is immensely potent and pervasive. Put this in your favorite salad dressing, or gently brush a peeled clove of garlic on some freshly toasted French bread, and you will soon learn how much or how little garlic you like. Otherwise beware of the use of raw garlic, except in a garlic sauce—and avoid serving garlic sauce to anyone who is not an avowed garlic lover. It is potent, health-giving, and greed-rousing—but it is well to be able to spend the next twenty-four hours in the great outdoors, unless you continue in the company of garlic eaters. Garlic sauce, incidentally, is dear to the Greeks. I first met it in a Greek restaurant in New York, appropriately and phonetically listed as "Gollic Sauce." You can imitate it by adding to a cup of mashed potatoes about a third of a cup of good olive oil, the same amount of sour cream and two or three cloves of garlic put through the garlic press. Keep it hot in a double boiler. It won't last long—especially if you serve it with broiled eggplant slices, followed by slices of bread to take up the slack.

Most cookbooks, as has been noted on an earlier page, give the impression that you can toss garlic into hot fat as you would onion. This is a delusion. Garlic burns in hot fat, and gives off a foul stench. Put it, instead, in butter or whatever fat you use, over a low flame. Cook it gently, and stop before it gets brown or black. If you wait until there is liquid other than fat in the pan, you can safely put in the garlic and let it cook ten to twenty minutes. Cooked too long, garlic loses most of its flavor.

Garlic cloves in Cellophane packages are usually tired. Better buy fresh garlic by the bulb, or two or three bulbs at a time. Each bulb has from fifteen to twenty cloves or sections. Garlic seasoning or powders should be viewed with suspicion. The real article is cheap and better. It can be bought in most groceries or vegetable markets patronized by persons of Italian, Spanish, Portuguese or Greek origin.

Herbs: Their Use and Abuse

Herb cookery has been so blown up as a fad in recent years that many cooks without gardens and without experience with herbs are shy about using them. Furthermore, amateurs sense that fresh herbs have much to commend them over dried herbs, and they suspect correctly that it is hard to find fresh herbs other than parsley.

Yet herbs are not luxury goods, nor is their use hard to learn. They play a big part in good cooking. If, besides chives, which are usually classed as an herb, you can have parsley, chervil and marjoram or basil, you will be able to perform miracles in the kitchen. If, in addition, you can acquire or grow fresh tarragon, you will be fortunate indeed. Of the others, rosemary, thyme and oregano (which is close kin to marjoram, but much more potent) are the ones most often called for. Good markets in large towns and cities are likely to carry some or all of these in season. Many other herbs are described in herb cookbooks. But however important they may be for certain dishes, most cooks need them rarely. Why not leave the more esoteric use of the rarer herbs to hobbyists?

A few words about the commoner herbs:

PARSLEY is the least obtrusive in flavor and the most decorative in appearance. Even when used as a garnish it should be eaten, not only for its taste but because of its richness in vitamins and iron. Chopped, it is indispensable in anything requiring what the French call *fines herbes*—a combination of fresh herbs used for seasoning omelets and sauces. Parsely is an ingredient in many good dishes. If you buy it in the market, you can keep it several days by putting its feet in water.

CHERVIL is a particular favorite of the French. It resembles parsley in appearance but has a sweeter flavor. The French use it commonly in recipes calling for *fines herbes*. Chervil is not widely used in the United States but can easily be grown from seed. It is particularly good in salads and egg dishes.

MARJORAM likewise is excellent in *fines herbes*, and enhances egg dishes and sauces. But go gently with its cousin, oregano, which looks to be its twin but which is so strong and pungent that even a tiny bit will give a sharp flavor to a spaghetti sauce.

TARRAGON is wonderful with eggs, fish, tomatoes and salads, and also is indispensable in any combination of *fines herbes*. A tablespoon of chopped tarragon will go far. If you are tarragon-wealthy, stew a fistful of it in clear broth for twenty minutes, strain it, and you will have a soup which is hard to beat.

BASIL, like marjoram, for which it can often be substituted, is good in eggs and salads.

THYME is fine in poultry stuffing. Use it sparingly in anything else.

ROSEMARY is good in soups and stews. Otherwise be cautious.

OREGANO is favored by Italians in many dishes. Incidentally, they pronounce it o-RAY-ganno. It is a must —in very small amounts—in many sauces to accompany a pasta, but, as indicated above, it is so dominant that it is likely to kill other flavors. Use only a tip of the new growth.

Dried Herbs

The difference between fresh and dried herbs, apart from a certain distinctiveness of flavor, lies in the quantities which you will use. Most fresh herbs are more pervasive than their dry counterparts. But much depends on how well and how recently the dried herbs have been put up, and the extent to which they have been fortified. No rigid proportion of dry to fresh herbs can be suggested. Here again, the best rule is to experiment. Try, beginning with too little. Let your own likes determine the amount that you finally decide to use.

Spices

Under this heading are usually classed not only such true spices as cinnamon, nutmeg and cloves, but also ginger, mustard, the various kinds of peppers and other similar dried and usually powdered or ground articles with marked flavors.

With the exception of mustard and the peppers, these are used primarily in desserts and cakes. All—including the peppers—should be used sparingly. If you like pepper, buy a small pepper mill. Fresh-ground black pepper as a rule is better than factory-ground. If you are curious about the "red" peppers, be sure to distinguish between cayenne and paprika. The former, if of good make, is so hot that even an eighth of a salt spoon is likely to overflavor a dish. Paprika, on the

The Art of Seasoning

other hand, is so mild that it hardly deserves to be classed with the peppers. Beware of the small, dried chili peppers, most of which come from Mexico. They can be dangerously hot and irritating, although when pulverized they may be useful in highly seasoned Mexican dishes.

Bottled Seasonings

It would be wrong to say that bottled seasonings, such as Worcestershire, Tabasco, and other popular items, have no place in the kitchen. But they should be used with caution. Each has a dominant flavor which tends to obliterate all other tastes.

More useful are soy sauce and monosodium glutamate, both of which are of Chinese origin, brought in by way of Japan. The last named, which is sold under numerous trade labels in this country, seems primarily to point up other flavors rather than to add a special flavor of its own. But it should be used in small quantities. A half teaspoon in a quart of soup is usually plenty, and a quarter of that amount will be enough for four eggs to be scrambled or made into an omelet.

Soy sauce is called for in many Chinese and Japanese dishes, and, if used cautiously, is often a good substitute for Worcestershire.

Tabasco is made of the hottest peppers. Take warning.

Other Seasonings

Under this head may be mentioned articles which, while useful as seasonings, also serve other purposes. These include lemon juice, vinegar, tomatoes and tomato extracts, anchovies and certain cheeses.

LEMON JUICE. This works wonders in many dishes. A few drops in a clear soup give it a tangy taste. It is a main ingredient in hollandaise, and is used in many other sauces. If you are lucky enough to be able to get a delicate lemon such as the Meyer lemon, widely grown on the West Coast, it will help you make delicious salad dressings. Incidentally, lemon juice added with discretion will point up dishes in which there is a good deal of butter or other fat, and, at the same time, will make these dishes more digestible.

VINEGAR. Most of the cheaper vinegars are so-called malt vinegars. Some of them can be of high quality, but nearly all of them are so bitter and strong that they must be used with restraint. As a rule wine vinegars are preferable, although some of these, under the influence of commercialization, have been degraded so that they are little better than malt vinegars. Wine vinegars often are seasoned with garlic, or with tarragon or basil or mixed herbs. It is a matter of taste which you should use. In reduced quantities good vinegar can replace the functions of lemon juice as outlined above. Vinegar also is useful in the cooking of certain tough meats. It is commonly used in salad dressings. To assume that you cannot afford a first-class vinegar is false economy. If you will add up the small quantity that you use in a week, even if you serve salad freely, you will find that it costs little more than a cent or two a serving. The difference in flavor in a dressing—or anything else—in which vinegar is used is very noticeable between top quality and cheap products.

TOMATOES. Deservedly these are among the most popular of all vegetables used for flavoring. The fresh are preferable to canned, but most canned tomatoes more nearly approximate the fresh than do any other canned vegetables. There are also good tomato concentrates. Of these tomato juice is the mildest, tomato paste the strongest and so-called tomato sauces in between. All serve useful purposes, but beware of the paste. Its taste is so trenchant that it can easily spoil a dish. Tomatoes have endless uses as seasoning. One can make fine sauces for pasta with them; they go well with rice in different forms; they belong in the sauce which accompanies a Spanish omelet; they perk up stews and dull casseroles. But leave tomato catsup to lunch counters.

ANCHOVIES. Either in the form of anchovy paste or of anchovy fillets (in cans) which can easily be chopped or mashed, this strongly flavored fish adds pungency to sauces and salad dressings. As anchovies in both forms are highly salted, allowance for this fact should be made. Try them in a sauce with spaghetti. Fillets cut up into half-inch lengths go well in mixed salad.

CHEESES. Among the cheeses used for flavoring or in cooking, the two most versatile are Italian—Romano and Parmigiano, or Parmesan. Kept until hard and dry, these grate easily. One or the other is a must with most pasta and rice dishes. Various adaptations of the English Cheddar are also much used. These go well in the making of cheese sauces, or in flavoring a casserole of macaroni. The quantity used of any of these cheeses is a matter of taste, and of the particular sharpness of the particular cheese used. If you want a mild cheese try a Monterey Jack or a Dutch cheese, preferably an Edam or Gouda, both of which are packed to look like cannon balls encased in red.

WINE IN COOKING

Cooking with wine has come to be regarded as a rather specialized branch of the culinary art. This is a mistake. There is nothing complicated about it. So

The Art of Seasoning

long as you bear in mind that the use of wine in cooking is to add to or to point up flavoring, you will find that recipes which call for wine are as easy to follow as others. Dry wines are most commonly used. This is true even in the use of sherry and Madeira. You are more likely to need white wine than red in your cooking.

In certain dishes wine is used in the actual cooking process—as, for example, some types of sole, some risottos, or in various meat casseroles. In others the wine is added just before serving, as in a Newburg sauce or a mushroom soup. Most recipes specify only small quantities of wine—from two or three tablespoons to a half cup. One of the main exceptions to this is the boiling of a ham or corned beef in wine, which necessarily requires large quantities. As the flavor contributed by the wine in this process is only incidental, it is safe to use cheap wines.

Not so, however, in using white wine in the cooking of fish, or in a cheese fondue, or sherry in a soup or Newburg sauce. It may be generalized that the less wine called for, the better should be its quality. To attempt wine cookery with poor wine is futile. The same is true when brandy is used. Rarely does a recipe prescribe more than a couple of tablespoons. Use a real cognac, if you have it. The extra cost will be trifling compared to the same volume of that abomination known as cooking brandy.

It would be possible to continue for pages listing seasonings. Even mastery of the detailed points set forth in the foregoing pages cannot, by itself, insure wise use of seasonings. Each person must experiment, and try all sorts of combinations. No branch of cooking needs greater attention. None, in fact, is more important when it comes to the production of really good food. If you will bear in mind the oft-repeated principle, "Don't overdo," you will be on the road to the acquisition of culinary wisdom. But be bold. Try combining flavors. Make tests to determine how much of a particular seasoning you find agreeable. And on those off days when every dish seems stale, flat and unprofitable, reach for your garlic press and begin by adding a half drop of garlic juice. Garlic fanatics insist that garlic is even good in ice cream. But members of the American Garlic Society, of which I am one, are of the opinion that one should draw the line somewhere. If I can have garlic in hors d'oeuvres, soup, the main course and salad, I'm prepared to pass it up in ice cream.

SOME 4

SAUCE SECRETS

Sauces may be divided into four main categories, of which the first three are cooked, and usually are served hot: (1) Sauces part of whose essential ingredients derive from the preparation of the dish with which they are to be served. Some of these resemble what are commonly called thickened gravies. (2) Sauces in which a dish is cooked, either in whole or in part, as, for example, the cheese sauce in which a macaroni dish may be baked, or the sauces in which the French finish cooking certain kinds of sole and other fish. (3) Sauces not made with any of the ingredients of a dish, but served separately to accompany it, such as hollandaise sauce to go with asparagus or cauliflower, or a polonaise sauce poured over a cauliflower. (4) Uncooked sauces, as, for example, a mayonnaise sauce. There are also uncooked sauces in which sour cream is the base and to which various seasonings are added.

EXTRACTIVE SAUCES

Let us begin with consideration of the sauces in which the ingredients of the dish with which they are served are to be incorporated. An obvious example of this is the use of the drippings in a roasting pan in which meat or poultry has been cooked. In using any of this extracted material it is usual to begin by skimming off all or most of the fats which have been exuded by the meats, or added in the process of basting. The roasting pan is then placed on a medium fire and a half cup of hot water is added to it. With a wooden spoon —preferably one with a flat edge—the entire bottom of the pan is then scraped, so as to incorporate in the liquid the little lumps of cooked meat juices which are in the pan. Ordinarily the resulting mixture is rich and full of flavor. Some sauces call for the cooking of ingredients such as chopped onions or mushrooms in a small amount of fat in the roasting pan. An example of this is a sauce to accompany a special chicken dish which we make from time to time. When the chicken

Some Sauce Secrets

has been browned and cooked with the addition of a half cup or more of white wine, it is removed to a hot dish. Two or three tablespoons of finely chopped shallots are then sautéed in the pan. A half cup of white wine is added as the shallots begin to assume a golden color. At this stage the same process is followed which was described above—a wooden spoon is used to scrape loose all the remnants of cooked juices which adhere to the bottom and sides of the pan. When this has been thoroughly mixed in with the white wine and shallots, the yolks of three eggs are beaten into a half cup of whipping cream and added to the pan. This should be done with care, and the moment the sauce begins to thicken it should be removed from the fire and kept warm. The dish is finished by pouring over the chicken a quarter of a cup of brandy, and lighting it. When it has burned out, incorporate the sauce with the burned brandy and spoon the mixture over the pieces of chicken to be served.

Another basic type of extractive sauce is used if a creamed cauliflower is to be served. The cauliflower is steamed in a covered pot on a rack over about a cup of water. It should not be too heavily salted. When the cauliflower is done, the water in which it was steamed is used instead of milk in the making of an ordinary white sauce, the details of which are outlined below. It has the merit of bringing to the sauce a pronounced flavor of cauliflower.

COMPONENT SAUCES

The second group of sauces—those in which a dish is cooked either in whole or in part—can best be understood after a brief consideration of the basic methods of preparing sauces.

ROUX—THE BASIS OF MOST SAUCES

Nearly all cooked sauces have as their foundation a combination of flour and butter in equal parts. This serves as a binder, and helps to make the end product smooth. The French call this a *roux*. They distinguish between three kinds of *roux*: (1) the brown *roux*; (2) the blond *roux*; and (3) the white *roux*. The difference derives from the extent to which the flour is cooked in the butter, although there is a school of experts the members of which hold that a brown *roux* should be made with flour which has been browned in the oven before being added to the butter. Ordinarily a brown *roux* is made by slowly cooking the flour in butter, stirring it constantly until it becomes brown.

The brown *roux* is used primarily for some of the

thicker and more elaborate sauces which the French make to accompany meat and game. You will find details of these in various cookbooks.

THE VERSATILE WHITE SAUCE

Many of the most useful sauces are—or can be—made with the white *roux*, which is the basis of what is commonly called a white sauce. A cup of this sauce calls for a tablespoon of flour, a tablespoon of butter and a cup of milk—together with some salt. When the butter is melted, the pan is removed from the burner while the flour is thoroughly mixed into the butter. The pan is then returned to the burner, and the *roux* is cooked gently for two or three minues and removed again. The milk is then added. If it is cold, pour in a quarter of a cup to begin with, stirring vigorously, and return the pan to the burner. As the sauce begins to thicken, add the remainder of the milk, stirring constantly with a wooden spoon. When the entire cupful has begun to bubble, let it cook very slowly for at least ten minutes, so that the ingredients will be well blended. The secret of making a good white sauce—and most other sauces—is to cook it slowly, stirring constantly. For this there is no substitute or short cut.

If you fail to stir and watch it, the sauce will not blend smoothly and part of it may burn.

The character of this basic white sauce can be changed by substituting some other liquid for milk. Among those commonly used are soup stock, the water in which a fish has been poached, wine (preferably white), tomato juice, or a combination of two or more. The procedure is the same, whatever liquid is used. Other seasonings may also be added, as, for example, cheese. A cheese sauce, as already indicated, can be effectively used in a dish of baked macaroni. If you will look over some of the recipes for sole as the French cook it, you will see that many of them call first for poaching the fish in a small amount of fish stock or wine or both, and then reducing the liquid in which the fish has been cooked and mixing this liquid with a white sauce or one of its variants. It is obvious that in this manner some of the delicate flavor of the fish is incorporated into the sauce.

Another way to change the character of sauces is, before adding flour to the butter, to cook in the butter for from three to five minutes either finely chopped shallots, or grated or very finely chopped onions, or cut-up mushrooms—to name three of the most obvious and most often used ingredients. As soon as these have

Some Sauce Secrets 43

cooked for a few minutes the flour is added, and then whatever liquid you plan to use. It is obvious that this opens new prospects for flavoring a sauce.

SOME MUCH-USED SAUCES

Volumes have been written about the making of sauces. There are literally hundreds of different sauces made in France alone. Of these the best known are: béchamel, which is what we would call a white sauce with the addition of a teaspoon or less of finely minced onion; the velouté, which is a white sauce made by adding veal stock to the white *roux*; the chicken velouté, in which chicken stock is used instead of milk; the soubise sauce, which is made by adding a white sauce to a cup of chopped onions which have been parboiled for a few minutes and then sautéed in butter until they are a golden color; the Mornay sauce, in which egg yolks and cream, together with grated Parmesan or Swiss cheese, are added; and the poulette sauce, in which mushrooms and shallots are cooked and added to a white sauce.

INDEPENDENT SAUCES

Among the sauces which are not made with any of the ingredients of the dish with which they are to be served, the most important is hollandaise. This has long had a reputation for being hard to make. We have never had trouble when we follow the recommendation contained in numerous cookbooks that the butter be divided into three equal parts. The first third is put in with the egg yolks and other ingredients. The second is added when the first has been dissolved, and then the third is added. It is important not to attempt to make a hollandaise over too high heat. It should be made in a double boiler, but should not stand at any time over boiling water. Like almost all sauces it is the better for being slowly made.

Incidentally, when whipped cream is added to a hollandaise it becomes what is called a mousseline sauce, which has the advantage of going further and yet having the same excellent flavor as hollandaise. It is often served with hot asparagus. The process is simple. Beat two tablespoons of whipping cream for each cup of hollandaise to which it is to be added and then mix it thoroughly into the hollandiase.

We make a sauce which is kin to a hollandaise but is not so rich. Its base is four tablespoons of butter, into which go three tablespoons of lemon juice—preferably the juice of the Meyer lemon, which grows in gardens in most parts of California and which is less acid than

Some Sauce Secrets

most of the lemons on the market. If this is not available, reduce the quantity of lemon juice from three to two tablespoons. In a separate bowl beat the yolks of two eggs with a third of a cup of whipping cream. Into this put a half teaspoon of salt, a quarter teaspoon of monosodium glutamate and—most important of all—a small clove of garlic crushed in the garlic press. There should be about a half salt spoon of crushed garlic— no more. This mixture is then poured slowly into the melted butter and lemon juice, which are first given a whirl with the beater, and the whole is then slowly heated over a low fire, beating constantly with an egg beater until it thickens. Be sure to scrape the sides and bottom every half minute, more or less, so as to get an even thickness to the sauce. When done, it should be of the consistency of a regular hollandaise. For want of a better name call it Sauce Point of Whales. It is one of the best accompaniments to asparagus, broccoli, artichokes, boiled salmon and any number of other dishes with which a hollandaise would normally be served. We find, furthermore, that we rarely make enough to satisfy the hunger of guests and relatives.

In all of the foregoing sauces—and be it noted that I have mentioned only a very few of those most commonly used—the principles about varying the seasoning which were outlined in the preceding chapter apply with special pertinence. A touch of garlic, a bit of wine, a little condensed meat stock—the French call it meat glaze, or *glace de viande*—will completely change the character of any sauce. There is no fixed rule as to what to do. Experiment and try things for yourself. Don't forget that in the final analysis your likes and your family's likes should be the deciding factor.

TO THICKEN A SAUCE

The thickness of a cooked sauce deserves attention. One of the purposes served by adding liquids slowly to the *roux*—the flour cooked in butter—is to be able, at least in part, to control the thickness of the sauce which you are making. Most sauces should not be too heavy. Certainly they should not be thin and runny. If you add the liquid slowly to the *roux*, bearing in mind that as it cooks it will continue to thicken, you will soon learn to adjust a particular sauce to the needs of the particular dish with which you plan to serve it. Should a sauce turn out to be too thin, you can thicken it by adding slowly small quantities of *roux*, or, if you prefer, by adding the yolk of an egg, or two or three, thoroughly beaten up. The normal procedure is to beat the yolk or yolks and then add to this a small quantity—

say a quarter of a cup—of the sauce which you are making and beat again. You can then pour the mixture of beaten egg yolks and the small quantity of sauce into the main body of the sauce, stirring vigorously. Be sure that it does not boil after the eggs have been added, as they will then cook and disintegrate and the sauce will be spoiled.

UNCOOKED SAUCES

Almost all of the sauces in this category are served cold. Of these probably the most important and useful is mayonnaise.

Mayonnaise

Although this is primarily an adjunct to salad, it is good with cold vegetables such as asparagus or artichokes. It is also delicious with shrimps, raw carrots or cauliflower served as hors d'oeuvres, or to accompany a dish of cold salmon. Until the development of electric blenders, the making of mayonnaise was a difficult, long and often perilous process. In a cookbook published in New York in 1867, the author, a Mr. Blot, recommended placing the bowl in which the mayonnaise was to be made, on ice, and started out by directing that you should "commence stirring with a box-wood spoon, or, what is still better, a stone or marble pestle," and insisted that you should "stir without interruption, always in the same way and describing a circle. . . ." The oil was to be poured in drop by drop—two bottles of it in all. Later authorities prescribe different temperatures and methods, but emphasize the uncertainties and peculiarities of mayonnaise, not only in the making but when done. No wonder it long continued to terrify cooks. But with a Waring Blendor it takes literally less than two minutes. My wife, whose mayonnaise has won wide praise, has adapted the instructions issued with the blender by varying the contents, but not the procedure. She begins with an egg, a tablespoon of lemon juice and a like amount of tarragon wine vinegar, a half teaspoon of salt and an eighth of a teaspoon each of monosodium glutamate, basil seasoning powder, tarragon seasoning powder and a locally made seasoning salt, to which is added a squish of garlic from the garlic press. Into this is poured a quarter of a cup of oil (she uses olive and soy oil in equal proportions). The blender is then run for about fifteen seconds. The remaining three quarters of a cup of oil is added slowly, and the blender run for a few seconds after each addition. As the sauce gets heavier it tends to stick to the sides, and should be scraped off. To assemble the ingredients and

Some Sauce Secrets 49

to remove the sauce from the blender usually takes longer than to make it.

The difference in flavor between a homemade mayonnaise, like the above, and factory-made products is great —so much so that if you have a blender and have ever made your own, you will never again be content with the manufactured variety.

Vinaigrette

Another sauce used with salads or cold food is vinaigrette. This is little more than a somewhat sour French dressing (see page 164) to which may be added cut-up herbs or chopped hard-boiled eggs, together with chopped capers. Recipes differ. It is close kin to a ravigote sauce, or a remoulade sauce. In the latter is added a half cup of finely chopped sour pickles and a substantial amount of mayonnaise.

One of the most useful and popular cold sauces we know is one which we developed, and which does not seem to be even approximated in any of the cookbooks which I have examined. We call it a ginger-mustard sauce. It is made by mixing a heaping teaspoon of dried mustard with a level teaspoon of powdered ginger, a half teaspoon of monosodium glutamate and a teaspoon of a locally made product sold under the name of Seasonsalt, which appears to be a combination of vegetable extracts with table salt. While this Seasonsalt improves the flavor, it is not indispensable in the making of this sauce. Into the dry ingredients are put at least four drops of the juice of a clove of garlic, a half teaspoon of Worcestershire sauce and a half teaspoon of cold water. When a paste has been formed, add a half cup of sour cream. We use the processed kind. The sour cream and other ingredients are then thoroughly mixed and a tablespoon of chopped capers is added. The sauce can stand in the refrigerator until ready to serve. It is excellent with ham, cold cuts, shrimps served with cocktails, and many other dishes which are improved by a somewhat nippy accompaniment. Incidentally, by increasing the proportion of sour cream the sauce can be made milder.

THE CREAMED BUTTERS

Although, strictly speaking, the combinations of various ingredients with soft—not melted—butter are not sauces, they are often used to enhance the flavor of dishes. Among the ingredients thus worked into butter are cut-up fresh herbs, or a few drops of garlic juice, or some anchovy paste. One of the best known of such "sauces" is the so-called maître d'hôtel butter, which is made by adding lemon juice and chopped parsley to butter. The process, called "creaming," is easy if you take the butter out of the refrigerator an hour or more before it is to be manipulated. When you are ready to add whatever ingredients you plan to use, work the butter with a wooden spoon in a small mixing bowl until it is soft, and then add the ingredients and mix them thoroughly into the creamed butter.

THE IMPORTANCE OF SAUCE MAKING

Next to the art of seasoning, the art of making sauces is the most important of all branches of cookery. It is even more difficult, as the making of a sauce requires close attention throughout the entire process. Mere seasoning, in contrast, is usually a short operation, which is completed when the desired flavor has been achieved. If a sauce is neglected at any stage, it may spoil or turn into something of only indifferent merit. But there are few branches of cookery which are more universally appreciated when successfully carried out. No bottled or manufactured sauce equals a really good home-brewed sauce made with knowledge, seasoned with tact and served with good food.

THE CHALLENGE 5
OF THE EGG

In Europe eggs are comparatively scarce. American hens in 1952 laid almost 60 billion eggs. This was enough for about 1,330 eggs for every household in the country in that year. No wonder eggs are among the best liked of American foodstuffs.

Yet few foods are prepared in the United States with less imagination. Most cooks in restaurants think of eggs in only four forms: boiled, poached, fried or scrambled. Usually eggs are served unseasoned. Yet, soft-boiled eggs excepted, the possibilities of varying egg dishes are limitless, and many of the variants require no more time to prepare than does the cooking of plain unseasoned eggs.

FRIED EGGS

Consider fried eggs. As indicated in Chapter I, fried eggs can be produced with many delectable flavors. The trick is simple. After sliding the eggs into a little butter, or whatever fat you use for frying eggs (and remember, the less fat the better), add a tablespoon of hot water to the pan. Lower the heat as soon as the water steams, and cover the pan. The eggs will cook gently and quickly. Instead of being hard and leathery, they will be tender.

Different flavors are obtained by adding different seasonings to the water. For example, a drop of garlic juice in the water will perk up any eggs. If you have soy sauce, add a dash or two of this instead of garlic. Or try a tablespoon of tomato juice, or well-seasoned soup stock, or wine, instead of water. It is possible to make endless combinations of seasonings. Incidentally, we have found that eggs fried in a tablespoon of French dressing to which a little water is added are relished by guests.

SCRAMBLED EGGS

Scrambled eggs also lend themselves to many flavors. Chives, shallots or grated onion are always appreciated.

If you use the last be sure to put in only a very small amount—say a half teaspoon at the most. Raw onions are potent. Cut-up ham or bacon (cooked, of course) is also good in scrambled eggs. So is grated cheese—at a rate of a teaspoon or less for each egg. Try ripe tomatoes—about a teaspoon of tomato for each egg. They can be either cooked or raw, but if you use them raw, watch your mixture carefully as it may become watery, in which case the eggs may separate from the tomato. A few anchovies will give a dish of scrambled eggs a sprightly taste. A tablespoon of well-seasoned meat gravy can be effectively used. Mushrooms chopped and sautéed in butter go exceptionally well in scrambled eggs. Mix them into the eggs while the eggs are cooking. Caution: always cook scrambled eggs over a low heat.

POACHED EGGS

The best way of making poached eggs interesting is to pour good sauces over them. Sauces can be quickly made by starting with the traditional *roux*. (See p. 40.) This, as you know, consists of flour and butter, to which is added milk, soup stock or other liquid. You can incorporate almost anything which you have handy, and which you think would give the sauce a good flavor.

One of the best ways of using cheese with eggs is to

The Challenge of the Egg

make a cheese sauce. To do this, let an ordinary white sauce cool for a few minutes, and then add to it a half cup or more of grated American Cheddar, or whatever cheese you like which is not too strong. Stir this vigorously off the fire, and return it to a low burner, stirring until it just begins to bubble. It is then ready to be poured over the poached eggs on buttered toast.

An excellent variant of this cheese sauce can be made by substituting wine for the milk in the sauce. If you like this flavor, add a teaspoon of brandy to the finished sauce just before serving. If you stir it briskly, the brandy will help make the cheese sauce smoother.

Creamed tomato sauce is also easy to make. Add a drop of garlic juice to the tomatoes, and a bit of cut-up fresh herbs if available—preferably tarragon, basil or marjoram. You can also vary poached eggs by brushing with peeled garlic the toast on which the eggs are to be served. Do this before buttering the toast.

The poaching of eggs has been known to be the Waterloo of would-be cooks. This is hardly surprising in view of the conflicting directions in cookbooks. Some say that you must whirl the water in the pan so fast that, due to centripetal force, a single egg will remain tightly in the center of the pan. Not only is this hard to do, but it means that you have to poach each egg separately, which is a great time taker and a bore. Others counsel adding a teaspoon of vinegar, or salt, to the water, or a bit of wine. Any of these helps make the eggs set. We always put in a teaspoon of salt, or more. But the process of poaching will be simplified if you can get some of the now almost extinct tin rings such as our grandparents had in their kitchens. Occasionally you can find them in a hardware store. A friend made us some. As a result we can poach four or five eggs at a time in our frying pan without trouble.

THE ART OF THE OMELET

A branch of egg cookery which has been much abused in the United States is the making of omelets. Americans too often have accepted as the standard concept of an omelet the kind of leathery, puffed-up, tough dish served under that name in many dining cars and restaurants. This dish is usually overcooked and dry and tastes of burned eggs. It is made by separating the yolks from the whites, and beating the whites stiff and then putting them back in the mixture. The result bears no relation to the omelet as it has long been made in Europe. The true omelet is a French creation. There are a few simple tricks in making it. The best omelets are cooked in pans which are sacred to the omelet art. The ideal omelet pan is heavy, so as to distribute and retain the heat evenly. The sides should be rounded where they meet the bottom, so that the cooked omelet can the more easily be slid out of the pan onto the dish from which it is to be served. The pan should never be washed. Instead, wipe it with a paper towel. But do not despair of making omelets if you do not have a special omelet pan. Omelets can be made in an ordinary frying pan, but this requires care and constant watching, as most skillets heat unevenly or too fast. Be careful that parts of the omelet do not burn. Better to put it on low heat if you are using an all-purpose pan.

Whatever utensil is used, omelet making will be easier if you have a clear idea of how a French omelet should look. The outside should be firm, but scarcely browned at all. The inside should be as soft as underdone scrambled eggs. This consistency is easy to achieve if you add a tablespoon of water for each egg. Incidentally, the salt and other seasonings should be dissolved in this water, which is usually put in the mixing bowl before the eggs. The French, who hate egg beaters, insist that eggs destined for an omelet should be gently beaten with a fork. I have made hundreds of omelets. Always I have used a rotary egg beater, but have beaten the mixture for only a few seconds. I defy any Frenchman to detect from the taste or appearance that a beater, not a fork, has been used.

Omelets should be cooked in good butter—about a tablespoon per installment. The pan is ready to receive the omelet when the butter begins to brown. Caution: do not pour more than the equivalent of three eggs at a time into the pan. The reason for this is that if too much egg mixture is in the pan it is hard to cook the inside of the omelet enough without overcooking the outside. If, therefore, your recipe calls for more than three eggs, mix all the eggs with their seasoning, but cook the omelet in installments, adding butter to the pan before each installment. Quickly stir the eggs in the pan with a fork, and continue stirring and removing them from the bottom until they reach the consistency of soft scrambled eggs. This should take about a half minute—no more. Then let them set for ten seconds, and, with a spatula, begin folding them over. After ten years' experience I still have trouble transferring an omelet from the pan to the serving dish without breaking it. But one should be comforted by the fact that it will taste just as good if it is not in its perfect and pristine shape. It goes without saying that omelets should be eaten immediately. Few egg dishes lose their charm more quickly when kept waiting.

To list the things which can be put into omelets would fill a book. If you have fresh herbs, the making of what the French call an *omelette aux fines herbes* is a sure way of winning friends and gaining a reputation of being a good cook. At its best this dish ranks with the finest of all foods. For each three eggs add to the water a scant teaspoon each of chopped chives, chopped parsley and chopped tarragon. If you like marjoram, cut up only a few leaflets. As indicated in the preceding pages, begin with too little seasoning rather than too much. If the herbs are dropped into boiling or very hot water and can steep for a few minutes before being used, their flavor will be enhanced. A little experimenting will show that by varying the proportions of the different herbs, or omitting one or more and substituting others, you can produce excellent omelets with a somewhat different flavor from the one outlined above. If you do not have fresh herbs, try it with dried herbs, but be sure to let them steep. There are herb mixtures on the market prepared primarily for omelets and other egg dishes. Why not try one of them? If you can add to it a bit of a fresh herb such as parsley or chives, the resulting flavor is likely to be better.

One of the best variants of an herb omelet is made by using a heaping teaspoon of chopped shallots in place of chives. These are sautéed in the butter in the omelet pan until golden brown. We usually add in the water which goes into the eggs a generous teaspoon of chopped chervil or parsley. This mixture is then poured into the butter and shallots in the omelet pan and quickly stirred until sufficiently cooked.

Cheese omelets are excellent. Don't be put off by the fact that experts disagree as to how and when the cheese should be added. My own experience is that if cheese is put in the uncooked mixture it tends to stick to the bottom of the pan. Accordingly I sprinkle the grated cheese over the cooking omelet, just before it reaches the scrambled-egg stage.

If you want to produce an omelet dish which is certain to be admired as a main course for a luncheon, try an adaptation of an omelet which I had forty years ago in the restaurant Laurent in Paris. Start with a very soft plain omelet and put it in an oblong shallow baking dish which has been well warmed but not actually heated. Then pour over the omelet a cheese sauce such as has been described above, to which you have added a little of the omelet mixture or a couple of beaten eggs. Place the baking dish under the broiler until the sauce begins to brown. This needs close attention, because if you leave it too long, or your dish is too hot, the omelet under the sauce will cook too much and will become hard or leathery. Like so many things in the art of cookery, the exact timing can only be learned by experimenting. Don't forget that, even though stoves are largely standardized, most ovens are temperamental. Your cooking successes in many fields will increase with the years of your knowledge and experience of your own oven.

Another always popular omelet is the so-called Spanish omelet. Most recipes call for either mushrooms or peppers, or both. We usually have neither. We make our sauce (part of which is used to fill the omelet, and the remainder to pour over it) by cutting finely half an onion and sautéing it in olive oil till it begins to turn golden brown. To this is added a cup of cut-up fresh or canned tomatoes, about half a small clove of pressed garlic, and a third to a half cup of cut-up olives—preferably the green-ripe variety. Add salt and pepper to taste, and let it simmer or cook gently for about fifteen minutes. This is added to a plain omelet, as described above.

The French put a variety of things into omelets. These include potatoes, ham, bacon, chicken livers, various kinds of vegetables such as asparagus tips or artichoke hearts, onions or anything that happens to be handy. You will find many recipes for omelets in good cookbooks.

THE EASY SOUFFLÉ

What many persons consider as the most triumphant of egg dishes is the soufflé. This is easy to make if you follow a few simple rules. The dish not only is attractive looking, but is a fine way to make effective use of leftovers. The commonest kind of soufflé is made with cheese, but we have served excellent soufflés made with the remains of cooked eggplant, or fish dishes, or soups, or combinations of leftovers. One of the best soufflés we ever produced was made by combining onion soup and eggplant.

The first step in the making of a soufflé resembles the preparation of an ordinary white sauce. Start with a tablespoon of butter and a tablespoon of flour, and mix in a cup of milk. Don't forget to stir vigorously all the while so as to blend it smoothly. Mix into this the cheese or cut-up ham or whatever ingredient you plan to use in the soufflé. If you use soup or anything more or less liquid you should substitute this for an equal amount of milk in the white sauce, or the soufflé will be too wet. When the mixture is completed, let it cool a bit. Then separate four to six eggs. Be very sure that not even a fraction of a drop of the yolk of an egg gets into the whites. Beat the yolks until they are light and somewhat fluffy. Wash the beater, dry it thoroughly, and then beat the whites until they are stiff. Mix the yolks into the sauce first, and then fold in the whites. Pour the whole mixture into a deep, round baking dish, large enough so that the level of the uncooked soufflé will be at least one inch below the top of the dish. Put it in a 325-350° oven. Experts differ as to whether the dish should be greased. We have always used ungreased dishes and have left the soufflé in the oven for about thirty-five minutes. It is well not to peek until the time is almost up. Some authorities insist that you must stand the baking dish in a pan of hot water in the oven. If this serves a useful purpose I have failed to discover it.

The absolute must about a soufflé is that it be eaten immediately on being removed from the oven. The reason for this is that it starts to fall the moment it leaves the heat of the oven, and the steam inside the soufflé condenses. It follows, therefore, that if you plan to serve a soufflé it should be timed so that it will not be ready either before your guests assemble, or before they are through with cocktails. A soufflé waits for no man—nor woman either.

SHIRRED EGGS

Shirred eggs are sometimes called "baked eggs." They are prepared in special, shallow ovenware, either of Pyrex or other material (the heavy French and Belgian enameled ironware includes excellent shirred-egg dishes, some for one, some for two eggs). Plain shirred eggs are made by placing a teaspoon of butter in one of these dishes, and, when it is thoroughly melted, breaking an egg or two into it and dotting the top with butter. If not sufficiently cooked in a moderate oven in three or four minutes, place it under the broiler for a minute or less. An excellent variant of this, which I found in a Dutch weekly many years ago, is made by adding to the butter three tablespoons of half-and-half or whipping cream, together with salt and whatever other seasoning you like. While the cream is still cool place in it two or three thin slices of Dutch cheese and break the eggs over this. Put the dish in a cold oven, adjust the heat to 325° and cook until the eggs are set.

Another excellent variant of shirred eggs is made by placing in a shirred-egg dish a teaspoon of butter, and warming in this three tablespoons of cream. When the cream is lukewarm add a half teaspoon of lemon juice and stir vigorously as the cream begins to curdle and thicken. Then add salt, and about an eighth teaspoon of pressed garlic. When the cream approaches the boil over a low fire slide the eggs into it and place it in a 350° oven. At the end of two or three minutes (depending on how you like your eggs) spoon some of the cream over the top of the eggs and place the dish for a minute under the broiler.

EGGS STATIC

We gave this name years ago to a form of what the French call *"oeufs cocotte"*—eggs cooked in dishes which are placed in boiling water until the eggs are done. In this case, instead of being put simply in butter and cream, as the French so often do, the eggs are placed in a sauce which is made with a tablespoon of butter and a like amount of flour, into which is stirred a cup of strong chicken broth, flavored with basil seasoning powder, a salt spoon of ginger, a drop of garlic juice and a scant teaspoon of fresh chopped marjoram or basil. Two tablespoons of the sauce are poured into the bottom of each container, then the eggs, then another two or three tablespoons of sauce. The containers are put in a shallow pan with boiling water, and remain there until cooked (with the yolks still soft) or about six to eight minutes, depending on the heat of the sauce and the coolness of the eggs.

There are countless other ways of preparing eggs. You will find them in your favorite cookbook. There are also books devoted exclusively to the cooking of eggs. As this volume is not a book of recipes I suggest that you look for them elsewhere.

Even more important, look for fresh eggs. They still exist, despite the enormous quantities of eggs in cold storage. The problem is how to find them, unless you live in or near the country. For once I don't have any glib advice to give—except to keep looking and hoping, and, in the meanwhile, making the best of the eggs you can get.

BEAUTIFUL SOUP 6

For many Europeans soup is a full meal. Certainly it can be one of the best of dishes, rich in vitamins, minerals and proteins. Frugal French housewives are said to keep a kettle on the back of the stove into which they put the water in which vegetables have been cooked, and other odds and ends which may add nourishment and taste to a good soup. In fact, however, most French housewives, like most Americans, do not have a fire burning long enough to carry out this sort of soup making. But the idea is sound—that the French put things in soups which Americans waste. Certainly Frenchmen look on soup making as one of the chief functions of a good cook.

Americans have never been soup-conscious. This may

be due to the insipid nature of many of the so-called soups served in restaurants and at lunch counters in this country. Perhaps as a people loving short cuts we shun processes which cannot be quickly consummated. Most good soups are slow in cooking. This does not mean that the cook need spend much time over the soup. But the kettle must simmer for three to eight or ten hours for almost any soup of which the base is meat or poultry.

It takes no longer to make several quarts of soup stock than only one. Preparation of the meat is easy and quick. You don't have to go so far as to follow Mr. Blot's recipe in his cookbook published in New York in 1867, to which I have already referred, which starts with the admonition: "Take the hind legs of fifty well-skinned green frogs" and calls for simmering them for four hours. It is a sidelight on how social customs have changed that Mr. Blot recommended that the frogs' legs, after being removed from the soup, should be served the next morning for breakfast. Apparently great-grandpa hadn't been conditioned to Wheaties.

Soups are of several kinds: (1) meat stocks; (2) thick soups; (3) vegetable soups; (4) chowders; (5) canned soups; (6) dried soups.

MEAT STOCKS

Stock is the name given to basic soups like beef, chicken or turkey broth, or any other clear soup made by the long, slow cooking of the meat and bones of one or more kinds of animals. Experts differ as to how to make them. Most French chefs insist that to the meat and bones must be added some vegetables—usually a leek or two, a turnip, and a bit of celery or carrot or both. For years we followed this system, but now we make stock without the addition of salt or of anything else. Our butcher gives us four to five pounds of beef shank with a knuckle of veal, the total weighing about six pounds. While the substances extracted from the bones helps make a soup jell, and marrow adds flavor, the smaller the proportion of bones to meat the better will be the soup. Meat and bones are washed and covered with cold water in a kettle which holds between four and five quarts. The pot is placed over a hot fire and watched as it approaches the boil so that the scum which rises can be removed. At the first sign of actual boiling the fire is reduced to "low" or "simmer" on the electric stove, or to the lowest point on a gas burner. After skimming off additional scum two or three times the soup is left to simmer, covered and undisturbed, for at least eight hours. It is then strained and poured into Mason jars. The yield is about three and a half quarts of good, strong stock. Experts say that the quicker the stock is cooled the better the soup will be. This is not always easy to do, especially in warm weather. As soon as the jars are cool they should be placed in the refrigerator. The coating of fat on top of them serves as a seal. They can be kept for from six to eight days after cooking. What has not been used by this time should be boiled again for at least ten minutes, and then returned to the refrigerator after cooling. Stock also will keep for months in the deep freeze. Incidentally, it is a sidelight on the advantages of modern refrigeration techniques that this same Mr. Blot, from whose cookbook of 1867 I have quoted, warned that in summer soup would not keep more than one day, and that if the weather was stormy (by which he meant "thunderstormy") it would not keep even for twelve hours. Refrigeration was in its infancy after the Civil War. The weather has no effect on modern refrigeration.

CHICKEN STOCK

We follow a similar process of soup making if we have the remains of a chicken on hand. This is cut up, put in cold water and simmered for three or four hours.

Beautiful Soup 71

If the bones can be broken, all the better. The resulting broth is good either plain or as a base with which to make a creamed chicken soup.

THE USES OF STOCK

The usefulness of soup stock, whether beef or chicken, is not limited to the making of soups. There are constant calls for small quantities of soup stock for flavoring. Stock is a principal ingredient in many sauces. Furthermore, it is often required in the cooking of dishes. To date, as was made plain in Chapter I, I have come upon nothing which is a substitute for good homemade stock.

Home-brewed stock makes a good clear soup. Add salt and any kind of flavoring you like. We put in a teaspoon of lemon juice for a quart of soup, and a half teaspoon of monosodium glutamate. If you like garlic add about an eighth of a teaspoon of garlic from the garlic press and let it simmer for five to ten minutes. A tablespoon of sherry per cup, or, if you like it even stronger, a tablespoon of brandy added before serving, will go far toward pointing up the flavor of soup stock. Another way to vary soup stock is to add a bit of tomato sauce or paste (but not catsup). Be cautious with the sauce or paste, as the flavor of both is strong. The tops of fresh shallots or chives cut up and sprinkled over a clear soup are decorative and add a pleasant flavor.

THICK SOUPS

The term "creamed soup" is usually applied to any kind of soup that has been thickened. Theoretically the thickening should be done by the addition of heavy cream. But in practice most cream soups are made by starting with butter and flour, and then slowly adding the requisite amount of meat or other stock. Among other ways of thickening a soup is to cook potatoes in it until they are soft and disintegrating. If you do this, give the soup a whirl in the blender before finishing it, or force it through a colander or sieve, the better to mix the potatoes in the stock. Beaten egg yolks, with or without cream, can be used to thicken soups by pouring a small quantity of the hot soup into the beaten eggs, and then reversing the process, slowly pouring the eggs into the soup, stirring vigorously the while. Don't let too much time pass between adding the yolks and serving the soup, or the yolks will cook and curdle.

VEGETABLE SOUPS

The French make fine clear vegetable soups without the use of meat stock. In this country the development of electric blenders has made it possible to produce excellent vegetable-purée soups easily and quickly. The usual procedure is to cook whatever vegetables you wish to use in a small volume of water, and then to put them in the blender. Vegetables can be combined, like leeks and potatoes, or leeks and carrots, or onions and celery, or any kind of combination which happens to appeal. The possibilities are many. If you have extra stock on hand try cooking the vegetables in this instead of in water. When the blender has done its work thin the purée by adding milk or soup stock. Most such purées call for as much butter as you can spare. This way of puréeing soups is a modern time- and work-saving substitute for the old process of forcing cooked vegetables through a fine sieve or colander. Doubtless the best chefs in Europe would scorn it—until they tried it—but it certainly is an easy way to make the bases of many good soups.

One of the best and simplest of these is a purée of fresh or frozen green peas. For each package of the frozen peas or its equivalent of fresh peas, cooked in a small amount of water and puréed in the blender, add about a cup of milk or half-and-half. Season with a generous dab of butter. Be careful not to oversalt the water in which the peas are cooked. Cream of spinach can be made in the same manner, using a package of the frozen spinach. The same can be done with a package of frozen asparagus tips.

Another easy and good vegetable soup is a cream of fresh tomato. This is a summer soup. Cut up one large or two small tomatoes per person and put them in two tablespoons of butter per portion and a like amount of hot water in a deep pan. Let them cook slowly (covered) for about twenty minutes. Pass them through a sieve to get rid of the skins. Into the remaining liquid add whatever amount of milk or half-and-half you care to use, and such seasonings as you like. Among the things that go well with tomatoes are tarragon, a bit of garlic juice, black pepper and even a pinch of mace. Be generous with butter, as it helps to overcome the acidity of the tomatoes. If they are unduly bitter add a pinch of baking soda before putting in the milk. But avoid soda if possible, as it is said to destroy the vitamin values of fresh vegetables.

One of the most famous of vegetable soups is French onion soup. This also is simple to make. Directions differ. We slice thinly a large onion per person to be served, and put the lot in a pan with butter and olive oil in equal proportions. Allow a half tablespoon of each for every cup of soup. Cook the onions over a slow heat, so that they do not brown or burn. When they have softened and are beginning to yellow add a cup of stock for each person to be served. If they are onion-soup addicts, double the recipe. Let the soup simmer for twenty to forty-five minutes—the longer the better. We add salt, fresh-ground black pepper and a little lemon juice. If you want to serve an onion soup that will be much liked pour into each bowl a tablespoon of heavy cream and a tablespoon of brandy. Also rub with garlic the prescribed piece of toasted French bread which is placed in the bottom of each soup bowl. We sprinkle freshly grated Parmesan or Romano cheese over each bowl, but any other firm cheese which is not too strong can be used. Beware of little packages of grated cheese. Most of them are offensive.

A soup rarely made in America, but which ranks high on the lists of those few gourmets who have tried it, is a cream of garlic soup. The way we make it is to squeeze a good-sized clove of garlic for each bowl of soup into a tablespoon of butter per bowl, and let the garlic cook slowly in the butter over a low heat until it is softened. Warning: do not let it brown or burn, as this will spoil the taste. Add a scant tablespoon of flour for each tablespoon of butter. Let it cook for a minute or so, stirring constantly. Then add a cup of stock, preferably chicken, for each cup of soup you plan to serve—and into this put two or three sprigs of rosemary and of thyme, tied together. Add whatever seasoning you like. We put in about a salt spoon of powdered basil for every two cups, and a tiny pinch of ground cloves. Be sure to stir the soup constantly until it boils, so as to prevent the flour and butter from lumping. Then let it simmer for twenty to thirty minutes and strain to remove the herbs. If you can spare a tablespoon or more of whipping cream per cup, scald this and add it just before serving.

It is worth experimenting with fresh vegetable soups. Even lettuce makes a good soup—especially a head of romaine. Start by cutting up three or four shallots and sautéing them in butter for a few minutes. If you have no shallots, use a small quantity of grated onion. Shred the lettuce as if it were cabbage being cut up to make cole slaw. Rinse the lettuce and add it to the shallots. Stir it for a minute, then cover and allow it to steam for about five minutes. Add three quarters of a cup of stock for each portion to be made, and let it simmer for ten minutes. We like to add a tablespoon of cream or half-and-half per serving.

CHOWDERS

Strictly speaking a chowder is a soup made out of sea foods. Most Americans know clam chowder. In New

England fish chowders are justly popular. The Italian minestrone, although it bears no resemblance to chowder, is like it in that it contains a number of ingredients destined to be eaten before they are overcooked. In Hungary the Legation chef often made for me what I called a vegetable chowder. The process was simple. He took several vegetables and listed the time needed to cook each until just tender. Then, beginning with the one that took most time, he dropped them into boiling stock, each for its prescribed number of minutes, with the result that all would be properly cooked and ready to eat at the same moment. The soup or chowder was served promptly. The fact that soups thus made have the common characteristic that none of the vegetables is overcooked differentiates them from soups in which vegetables are cooked until soft or pulpy.

New Englanders are touchy about chowders. Even though they disagree as to what should go into a true chowder, they are as one in regarding the making of chowder as an inherited characteristic, which cannot be acquired by purchase, imitation or marriage. If it's not made by a New Englander, it's not a chowder—this is their conviction.

As my New England ancestry has been tainted by New York Dutch blood, and by having had a French grandfather, I cannot speak with authority about the making of chowders. Yet as one who loves chowder, whether fish or clam, I must risk the scorn of New Englanders by reporting that we have made fish chowder by using canned tuna. Unthinkable and unorthodox as this is, I shall detail its preparation for the delectation of Americans who live beyond the Atlantic shore line, and to whom fresh clams, or fresh haddock or halibut, are unavailable. Canned chowders have been put up by New England canners, but I would not offer one to a New Englander. As a descendent of Connecticut stock I always heard that there were people in that state who delighted in making and selling wooden nutmegs. I do not wish to slur chowder canners by making possibly unjust implications. But I know that wooden nutmegs were salable because the buyers wouldn't recognize the original if it were presented to them. Can it be thus with canned chowders?

We make our so-called chowder by using two cups of stock, or a cup each of water and milk, for every three persons to be served. Into this we dice a potato, an onion and some celery. When the vegetables are about half cooked (which is likely to be in about ten minutes) a can of tuna from which the oil has been drained is added. Let it simmer until the vegetables are cooked but still firm. Into this then go two tablespoons

Beautiful Soup

of hot cream per person. The chowder is served with pilot biscuits, saltines or Saratoga crackers. This is not, of course, a chowder according to Hoyle (or even according to Fanny Farmer) but it is a good fish soup which can easily be made if you live beyond the reach of fresh sea fish.

By using canned minced clams we make as good a clam stew as is served at the Oyster Bar in Grand Central Station in New York. This dish has the advantage of being easy and quick to make. As we like to serve it as a one-dish meal, with a large bowl per person, we use a can for each portion. Following the technique used at the Grand Central Oyster Bar, we start by melting a large pat of butter per portion. To this the clam juice is added, reserving the clams. By way of seasoning: celery salt, a dash of Worcestershire and some paprika. When the juice comes to the boil, two parts of half-and-half cream are added for each one of clam juice. When the liquid has again come to a boil the clams are added. The stew should not boil or stand long after the clams have been put in, or they will toughen. If we have cream to spare we add a tablespoon or more per bowl. Serve the stew with a generous pat of butter floating on top, and accompanied by saltines. This is a good replica of what the stewards at the Oyster Bar call "clamstoochoptaffcream."

CANNED SOUPS

Many persons swear by canned soups. Others dislike them. The rule regarding any canned soup is to accept it as an unfinished, precooked product which is not ready to be served until it has been properly seasoned. Don't blame the soup maker if you find his products dull as they come out of the can. Like all makers of canned goods, he has to err on the side of bland flavoring because he caters to mass tastes.

In the seasoning of canned soups be guided by your own likes. Among obvious things which can perk up a canned soup are wine, cream, butter, fresh herbs, garlic, onion juice or lemon juice. Most canned cream soups can be improved by adding milk. A canned black-bean soup is the better for the addition of sherry or a good light wine. We use soup stock to thin a canned split-pea soup. Do not take too literally the directions the soup makers put on the can. Use your imagination after tasting the product as it comes from the can, and think what might improve it.

DRIED SOUPS

Some good dried soups are exported from Switzerland and Germany. It is best to follow precisely the

Beautiful Soup

directions for transforming them from their dried to a liquid state. But when this has been done, taste the soup with a view to adding seasonings of your own. Try a bit of fresh vegetables or herbs, such as cut-up celery, shredded lettuce, parsley or cut-up shallot tops or chives. However excellent dried soups may taste, they cannot have all of the more life-giving nutritional values which fresh foods have.

ACCOMPANIMENTS FOR SOUPS

You will find full directions in cookbooks for many of the more formal decorations with which the French and other expert cooks like to beautify a dish of soup. Some of these need time to make, and are little more than frills. Among the simpler ready-made additions to clear soups are, as I have said above, chopped chives or tops of shallots. Many thick soups will taste better and look more attractive if chopped parsley or chives are scattered over each bowl or cup. Croutons of bread fried in butter, or in butter and olive oil, go well with thick soups—notably, tomato, split-pea and lentil soups. Try small squares of medium-cooked bacon in a black-bean or split-pea soup. Grated cheese is always served with onion soup and minestrone. Try it with other soups and see how you like it.

LAST WORDS ON SOUPS

The tradition in fashionable circles has been to regard soups as appetite whetters. Even the hard headed French, whether fashionable or not, look upon failure to serve a good soup at the beginning of a meal as culinary sacrilege. But soups, with the exception of thin broths, can be filling. It would not be surprising if an increasing number of American housewives would take a leaf from French country cooking and adapt the custom of making an entire meal out of a nourishing soup. Certainly there is much to be said for this time-honored way of combining meat and vegetables in a single tasty dish. If you try it, be sure to time the cooking of the vegetables so that none is overdone. You can stop cooking them when they are half done, and then resume it ten to fifteen minutes before the meal is to be served. No precise suggestions as to timing can be made, as much depends on the extent to which the soup cools.

The Book of Genesis states that the mess of pottage for which Esau sold his birthright was a soup of lentils. This altogether admirable one-dish meal is still a favorite in the countries bordering the Eastern Mediterranean. Although Jacob, who cooked the soup for Esau, doubtless used other ingredients and other methods of making the lentil soup which he gave his brother, Americans will find a lentil soup easy to make in a pressure cooker. The Greeks usually add onions, garlic, olive oil, a little vinegar, thyme, salt and pepper. Some of them also like to add cloves. The proportions vary with the taste of the individual. When we make lentil soup in a pressure cooker we add a cut-up onion, two cloves of garlic and three cut-up stalks of celery to a cup of dried lentils, in three cups of soup stock, to which two tablespoons of olive oil and a teaspoon of wine vinegar have been added. In about twenty minutes the lentils are sufficiently cooked. Pass them through a colander and you have a fine mess of pottage. Unquestionably Esau paid high for his soup, but a good lentil soup is worth the time it takes to make it, and will cost you only a few cents a cup.

FISH— 7
FINE FARE

Because wise men like fish it has often been said that fish nourishes the brain. Whether this is an old wives' tale or true, fish is among the best foods.

Early explorers and settlers in America were amazed at the number and kinds of fish in the waters of the Atlantic coast. The intrepid and fanciful Captain John Smith (of Pocahontas fame), in a book published several years before the Pilgrims landed at Cape Cod, told of the ease with which hundreds of fish could be caught by a single person in a day in New England waters. In words of which the author of *The Compleat Angler* would surely have approved, he wrote: "What sport doth yield a more pleasing content, and less hurt or charge than angling with a hook and crossing the sweet air from isle to isle over the silent streams of a calm sea?" A few years later, Francis Higginson, one of the first settlers in Salem, Massachusetts, described in a book about the wonders of New England the abundance of fish of all kinds along the New England coast. "I saw great stores of whales," he wrote, "and grampuses and such abundance of mackeral that it would astonish one to behold. Likewise codfish." He mentioned that it was common to take lobsters weighing up to fifteen pounds, and told of some weighing as much as twenty-five pounds apiece.

Three centuries of civilization—and, in particular, the last eight decades of industrialization—have gone far to cut down the former abundance of fish in American waters. Yet fish are still plentiful and are among the cheaper of good foods. Thanks to the development of deep freezing, frozen fish can be transported and stored as was never possible in earlier days.

Because most Americans live beyond the reach of fresh fish it is well to start with the uses of canned fish. I shall then touch on some of the frozen fish which are available in larger centers, and, finally, consider fresh fish.

CANNED FISH

A number of types of fish are good canned. Unfortunately the one put up in largest volume, salmon, has been canned with the least regard to preserving the excellent flavor of the original fish. Of canned salmon about the best that can be said is that it is nourishing, and is better than no fish at all. But if there are ways of making it palatable I have yet to come upon them. Several million ex-GI's, I am sure, agree with me about this.

Sardines, especially the imported varieties, which have been boned and skinned, are excellent in salads, and are also good when broiled and served on toast. They are comparatively expensive, and are likely to continue to be thought of in terms of picnic lunches and for cocktail canapés rather than as a main article of food.

Tuna is beginning to crowd salmon. It is an excellent canned fish, usable in many ways. In the chapter on soup I described a fish chowder with tuna as the base. Quick-lunch eaters have often been tempted by tuna salad—to their regret. But tuna makes a fine salad if served with a good dressing. We use either homemade mayonnaise (which, as you have seen in chapter IV,

Fish—Fine Fare

takes literally only two minutes to make) or mayonnaise mixed with an equal amount of sour cream. Too much dressing will drown the flavor of the fish.

Creamed tuna on buttered toast makes a good luncheon dish—quick and nourishing. Try adding a little lemon juice to the white sauce, and then simmering the tuna in the sauce for fifteen to thirty minutes. The flavor of the tuna will permeate the whole dish. Incidentally, a good variant of creamed tuna can be made without materially altering the basic flavor by adding a few tablespoons of cut-up fresh celery just before serving.

Some of the fish canners in Gloucester, Massachusetts, put up what they call fish flakes. These are combinations of haddock, cod and hake. We like the kind Davis cans. These fish flakes not only are useful for emergency dishes when unexpected guests arrive, but also are the bases for good fish hashes, and for creamed fish dishes to be baked in the oven. I have even used fish flakes following the general recipe for lobster thermidor, and produced a first-rate dish. Fish flakes in a Newburg sauce served with rice are also good.

If you want to experiment with a fish hash, take a can or two of fish flakes and add to it about an equal volume of cut-up cooked potatoes, with which chopped onions and celery have been mixed. A pleasant variant is to add a tablespoon of chopped bacon, which should be cooked only a little. Place the hash in the oven until browned. It is well to dot the top with butter. Fish flakes to which mayonnaise and sour cream are added also make a good salad in place of tuna. As the flakes have a less marked flavor than tuna you may wish to make the dressing sharper. This can be done by the addition of onion juice, or fresh tarragon leaves, or almost any kind of seasoning that happens to appeal to you.

Another canned seafood which we have found of value is minced clams. By way of caution it should be noted that not all brands are equally free from sand. We have had good luck with an eastern brand put up by S. S. Pierce & Co. in Boston, and with the Pioneer brand put up on the West Coast. As we live in California it is this last named which we ordinarily use.

If you are partial to codfish cakes—as nearly everyone with a New England background is—try one of the good brands, like S. S. Pierce or Davis. We mix into them not only a beaten egg or two, but some butter, a little cream, and at least a half teaspoon of onion juice and of Worcestershire per small can. It is easy to sauté or deep fry cakes made from this home-improved mixture. We sometimes put the entire mixture in a shallow baking dish and, after letting it cook in the oven a few minutes, brown it under the broiler.

FROZEN FISH

The deep freezing of fish has been one of the greatest contributions to modern nutritional progress. Many fishing boats are equipped to freeze fish within a very short time of their being caught. As a result, fish freshly caught and frozen are now available in many parts of the United States where hitherto it was impossible to buy them.

As the preparation of frozen fish for cooking resembles so closely that of fresh fish unfrozen, it is only necessary here to say that the instructions put out by the processors of frozen fish should be closely followed as to defrosting. Once they are unfrozen, fish of a particular kind can be treated just as would be fresh fish of the same species.

It is well to check with your dealer as to how long he has had frozen fish which you want to buy. The storage life of fat fish is shorter than that of lean fish. Some state laws require frozen fish products in markets to be examined for quality after one year. Others do not permit storage for more than a year. Samples of lean fish kept longer than this have been found to have their flavor unimpaired. On the other hand samples of fat fish—those with a higher oil content—have been found to undergo objectionable flavor changes within as little as six months. As it is so obviously to the interest of those who put up, as well as those who market, frozen fishery products to keep the customers satisfied, the likelihood of getting frozen fish which have passed their prime is small. It is the function of the processors to see that the fish are of good quality and fresh when placed in the freezer, and that they are properly frozen and carefully prepared for storage. In addition, they have to be properly cared for in shipment, and properly stored by the retailers.

FRESH FISH

Fresh fish are normally divided into two broad categories—those that come from salt water and those taken in fresh water. They may be further subdivided by classifying shellfish and crustaceans separately.

For our purpose a more subtle subdivision is advisable—fish which have a distinctive flavor and those which are more or less bland. A reason for this classification is that those with delicate flavor require greater care in cooking and are best with less seasoning than are the more bland or coarse fish. Among the best of

Fish—Fine Fare

the delicate salt-water fish are shad, bluefish, butterfish, sand dabs, salmon, whitebait and swordfish. Among the better known of the bland fishes are cod, halibut, haddock, sole, flounder and bass.

Before discussing these fish individually it should be emphasized that all fish must be very fresh and that no fish should be overcooked. Delicate fish are best when broiled. Brush them with butter before putting them under the broiler. They should not be placed too near the fire or broiling element—say, four to five inches from it. The side of a fish first exposed to the broiler requires longer to cook than does the other, for the obvious reason that the heat is transmitted from the side near the broiler to the other side. It follows that when the fish is turned over, the second side will be warmer than was the flesh of the fish when it was originally placed under the broiler. For timing consult the schedules in any cookbook. The thicker the fish the longer it will take to cook. Large fish like salmon, swordfish, Spanish mackerel and halibut are generally cut into steaks. These should be about three-quarters of an inch to one inch thick in order to yield the best flavor. All of these fish should be served with nothing stronger than melted butter and perhaps a dash of lemon.

The blander fish, like cod, halibut, haddock and sole,

lend themselves well to kinds of cooking other than broiling. They may be poached in a little water and wine, or what the French call a *court-bouillon,* which is a sort of fish-and-vegetable stock, usually with wine added. Recipes differ. Make your own choice. But cooks agree that in poaching fish they should not be allowed to boil. They should just simmer. Fish thus cooked in stock are usually served with seasoned sauces.

Sole is often thus treated, and is a favorite of gourmets. In fact, sole derives much of its repute from the manner in which it is disguised by skillful chefs. You will find recipes for sole calling for mussels, oysters, mushrooms, herbs, cheese, truffles and all kinds of fairly strongly flavored ingredients. Many of the resulting dishes are excellent, but the fish plays only a minor part in the flavor of the dish. I would suggest trying any French recipe for sole which appeals to you and substituting for the sole some of the canned fish flakes of which I spoke above.

The fact that nothing has yet been said about frying fish does not mean that this way of cooking fish is inferior to others. As a matter of fact, there are fish which are very good when fried. This is true of whitebait and abalone and it can be true of some of the flounder tribe like sand dabs. There are two principal ways of preparing fish for frying. One is to dust the fish with flour, or shake them in a paper sack in which a couple of tablespoons of flour and an adequate amount of salt have been put. The other is to dip them in batter. In some parts of the country the fish are rolled in corn meal. The exact procedure is comparatively unimportant. What counts is the kind of fat used, and its degree of freshness. Also its temperature. Butter used as cooking fat has too strong a flavor for the more delicate fish. So does olive oil. It is better, therefore, to use one of the blander fats such as a peanut oil or any vegetable oil that does not have a pronounced flavor. Oft-used fats can spoil the taste. If you use batter the oil should be hot when you drop the fish in—almost as hot as if you were deep frying. If you have dusted the fish with flour by shaking it in a paper sack, you do not need as high heat. Don't forget that whatever you do, you should not overcook your fish.

If you happen to have an infra-red broiler you will find it ideal for cooking fish. We do fresh salmon steaks in one of these, and know no better way of cooking salmon—including grilling it over charcoal. It is important to watch the timing as it is easy to overcook salmon or any other fish in one of these broilers. You would do well to examine closely the recommended heat and distance from the broiling unit which the makers advise.

Should you live near any part of the coast where fresh sardines are brought in to market, be sure to try them. As they are oily, it is well, if you grill them, to keep water handy to sprinkle over them, lest the fat flame and sear the fish.

Notice should be taken of one of the finest fresh-water fish that is to be found anywhere—the Lake Superior whitefish. Whitefish come from others of the Great Lakes and other fresh waters in the northern part of the American continent, but the extremely cold water of Lake Superior seems to give the whitefish taken in that lake a particularly desirable firmness and richness of flavor. Whitefish is best broiled. Unfortunately, the supply of whitefish is limited and it is rarely on the market except in the region of the Great Lakes.

Trout is the other best known and most popular of fresh-water fish. In the United States it is so scarce that you are not likely to come upon it except by chance —or through the kindness of angling relatives or friends. In Europe it is highly prized.

There are other fresh-water fish such as perch, sunfish and catfish, the cooking of which is a more or less

Fish—Fine Fare

localized accomplishment. Europeans serve—and like —carp. When disguised by a strong sauce it is edible. The average fish-loving American family is not likely to have many occasions to use any of these or other fresh-water fish unless a good local supply is near at hand.

SMOKED FISH

A few words about smoked fish: Smoked salmon can be good, but is expensive. It is useful as an hors d'oeuvre. On the West Coast smoked Alaska cod is sometimes available. This is one of the best of all smoked fish. Serve it steamed, with plenty of melted butter. Among others is finnan haddie, much of which comes from Nova Scotia. The basis of this is the haddock. It is excellent steamed and also makes a good creamed fish dish, in a white sauce. Its flavor is sufficiently marked to override the blandness of the white sauce. You will find that finnan haddie and kippered herring, which is a canned variety of smoked fish, are likely to be popular with the male members of your family. Most members of the second sex resist serving either because of the fact that their preparation—unless you have a powerful fan in your kitchen—means that the house will be fish-conscious for from twelve to twenty-four hours. I know of nothing besides the use of too much garlic which can cling more persistently to the atmosphere of a room than the cooking of kippers.

SHELLFISH

Of shellfish the main thing to be said is that oysters and clams are best when eaten raw, and still alive. Scallops, mussels and soft-shelled clams and the various crabs lend themselves to many excellent cooked dishes. Scallops are usually fried. Mussels, if you can find them (which is unlikely), are at their best in what the French call *moules marinières*. You will find recipes for this in various cookbooks. Oysters and both kinds of clams are, of course, excellent in stews. If you live within reach of fresh soft-shelled clams, try using some of the broth to make a thick white sauce and then poach some uncooked clams in this sauce. You are likely to find that this is a fish dish which you will be glad to repeat.

CRUSTACEANS

The crustaceans are a lordly tribe—lobsters, crabs, crawfish, prawns and shrimps. Unfortunately they are also expensive. They lose much of their delicacy of flavor when canned, and are not too satisfactory when

Fish—Fine Fare

frozen. Better buy them only if you live near salt water —and, if you want the best results, do not overcook them. There is no nobler sea food than a broiled lobster served with melted butter and a little salt. Unfortunately for the residents of the Pacific Coast the crustacean caught there and sold under the name of lobster is a crawfish, and lacks the delicate and distinctive flavor of the lobsters from the New England coast. By way of compensation, the large, hard-shelled crab of the Pacific is one of the finest sea foods. It is at its best steamed and served with nothing but salt and lemon juice. Prawns are excellent dipped in a bland batter and deep fried.

This does not mean that the more elaborate ways of serving these crustaceans are not tasty. Lobster, crab or shrimp Newburg can be delicious. But too often you are only dimly aware of the original delicacy of flavor of the crustacean you are eating. Lobster thermidor can be a great delicacy. But even though juices from the fish and from its shell go into its making, the sweetness of the lobster flesh is drowned by the seasonings in the sauce. Crab bisque is a magnificent dish, but the crab is not dominant, and so loses some of its distinctive flavor.

There is no point in cluttering up these pages with

detailed suggestions as to the preparation of particular fresh or frozen fish. The markets are so variable that, except in seacoast towns, you can rarely be sure of finding the particular fish you seek. By way of parting advice, don't hesitate to try fish that you have never tried before. Experiment, and remember three simple rules: (1) the fish must be very fresh; (2) it must never be overcooked; and (3) it should have a minimum of seasoning added, unless its natural flavor is insipid.

SIX HUNDRED MILLION 8
CHICKENS

To most Americans the words poultry and chicken are synonymous. Technically poultry includes turkeys, ducks, geese and squabs, as well as chickens. Yet few American families dine on duck once a year. They eat goose even less often. As for turkey—until the development of streamlined small turkeys after World War II, the eating of this delectable bird was usually confined to holidays. Squabs are a luxury, rarely served in American homes. But chicken is ubiquitous. Anyone who has been on a lecture tour in these United States is sure that the favorite food of all Americans is chicken, accompanied by gray mashed potatoes, and by pellet-like green peas. In actual fact, Americans eat 600,000,-000 chickens a year. While this is a staggering amount if laid out end to end, or balanced on top of the Washington monument, or in any other fanciful figure which appeals to graphic-minded statisticians, it comes to little more than a chicken a month for every family in the country. In view of the popularity of the bird it is surprising that more are not eaten.

Concentration on chickens has at least relieved housewives of the need of learning how to cope with other kinds of birds for the table. In Mr. Blot's cookbook of 1867, to which I have already referred, are recipes for cooking blackbirds, bobolinks, lapwings, meadow larks, rails, robins, thrushes, woodpeckers and yellowbirds. I was somewhat relieved to find that he classified as "seldom eaten" cranes, ostriches, peacocks and pelicans. He said that these were not so bad when young, but that when they were old, they were tough and "of a disagreeable taste."

WHY FRIED?

Ask the average American how he prefers his chicken, and the chances are that he will reply: "Fried, Southern style." Perhaps the popularity of fried chicken goes back to the childhood days of many Americans and their parents, when frying pan and Dutch oven were the chief cooking utensils, and almost all foods were fried—of which chicken was almost surely the most palatable. Good Southern cooks fry chicken in a skillfully prepared batter in fresh deep fat. This preserves the juices and the delicate flavors in the meat. Unfortunately, at least in most restaurants in the North and West, the technique is usually misapplied by persons who lack respect for good chicken flesh, and who use inferior batter and strong, old grease. The result is a travesty of the true Southern fried chicken. Northerners did not automatically acquire the art of frying chickens, Southern style, by winning the "War Between the States."

CLASSES OF CHICKENS

Chickens are usually classified according to size. Broilers weigh up to two and a half pounds, fryers between two and three and a half pounds, and roasters above three and a half pounds. In addition there are stewing hens and capons, which run to larger weights.

BROILERS, GRILLED AND BROILED

There is no better way to bring out the pure taste of a chicken than to grill a quartered broiler over charcoal. We have done it hundreds of times and never use any seasoning other than salt. We do not rub the birds with butter or oil, nor do we add herbs, or brush them with garlic, or in any other way try to modify the natural flavor. The quartered pieces are laid on the grill bone-side down, so that the heat first reaches this part of the bird. They should be turned several times so that they will be cooked through. The process usually takes from twelve to seventeen minutes, depending on the heat of the fire and the age and size of the bird. Experience will teach you the color and appearance which the skin has when the chicken is done. It should not be too dark brown, nor should it show signs of drying and puckering. We have found that if there is any doubt as to whether the pieces are cooked through, they can safely be left for two or three minutes more with the inside down and the skin side up. No further excessive cooking of the outside part will then take place.

To those who look upon grilling over charcoal as a process which is too complicated or costly, it should be pointed out that you do not need an expensive barbecue table or pit. Nor need the cooking be done outdoors. The one essential is a fireplace with a good draft. If you have this you can use one of several kinds of small portable grills which can be placed in the corner of the fireplace. A Japanese brand has recently been widely distributed. In California it sells for about fifteen dollars. It is big enough to hold a steak for four to six people. A broiler, quartered, may have to be done in two relays, if it is large. The best fuel is charcoal, but if this is not available, pressed briquettes can be bought in grocery or hardware stores. To start the fire I crumple two pages of newspaper and over this place a dozen bits of kindling about the thickness of a finger, and four to seven inches long. On this I pour a half cup of kerosene, and then place the charcoal on top of the kindling. I have a theory which I have not proved or disproved—that if kerosene is poured over the charcoal there is a residual flavor of the oil in the cooking.

If you do not have a grill you can broil chickens under the broiler in your stove. The main "out" about this method is that the intense heat generated by most broiler units tends to dry out the birds. If, therefore, you do them under a broiler, it is well to baste them every few minutes with butter. As the flame of the broiler is above the rack, rather than beneath as when cooking with charcoal, the initial position of the birds is reversed—i.e., the birds are placed on the broiling rack skin-side down, so that the heat reaches first the under part, or inside, of the chickens. They should be turned several times in the process of broiling.

BAKING BROILERS OR FRYERS

Another good way of cooking a chicken so that the flavor of the bird is at its purest is to place a broiler or fryer, which has been cleaned but not dismembered, in a shallow baking dish with three tablespoons of butter and a like amount of hot water. The chicken—which should be salted before cooking—is laid on its side and should be basted several times during a period of about thirty-five minutes in a 325° oven. It should then be turned and should be cooked and basted on the other side for an additional twenty-five to thirty minutes. It takes about a full hour to cook such a bird—depending on its weight and condition. If it is on the heavy side give it ten to fifteen minutes more in the oven. Do not be surprised if it is only golden brown in color. Birds done in this way are not expected to have the dark brown color of roasted chickens.

There are good variants of this way of cooking chickens. One is to place inside the cavity of the bird a few sprigs of rosemary. If you have tarragon, use a few stalks of this instead of the rosemary. If you have neither, crush a clove of garlic and rub it on the inside of the bird. Or substitute for the three tablespoons of water a like amount of white wine. All of these give a pleasant modification of the pure chicken flavor. Doubtless you will think of ways of your own for still further varying the taste. Try them, bearing in mind that there should be butter and liquid in the baking dish with which to baste.

CHICKENS IN CASSEROLES

If you make chicken casseroles you will probably find that it is best to sauté the chicken before putting it into the casserole dish. This means, of course, that it must be cut up so as to be easily handled. The sections should be dusted with a mixture of flour and salt. An easy way to do this is to put a half cup or less of flour, and a generous amount of salt, in a large paper sack, and shake the pieces briskly in the sack. Try a mixture of half olive oil and half butter for sautéing the pieces. Two to three tablespoons of each should be plenty, unless the volume of chicken is large. Remove the pieces when they are golden brown and place them in the casserole dish with a half cup of chicken stock. If there is enough fat left in the pan—say, two or three tablespoons—you might consider tossing into this some raw rice at the rate of a quarter cup per person to be served, and letting it fry for three minutes, stirring it constantly. This should not be put into the casserole until about thirty-five minutes before eating time. When the rice is added to the casserole there should be about two parts of liquid to one part of uncooked rice. If more liquid is needed to cook the desired amount of rice, add fresh or canned chicken consommé. As a variant, try a can of tomato juice. This will give the rice a pleasant flavor and will make a distinctly different casserole dish. If tomato juice is used, try adding a touch of garlic, or a teaspoon of Worcestershire, or some tarragon, or any other seasoning which you like with tomato. If there is too much liquid in proportion to the rice, remove some of it or leave the cover off the casserole. If the dish is too dry and you have no extra chicken stock on hand, try adding a little white wine to finish cooking the rice.

ROAST CHICKEN

Unless you have an electric broiler with a revolving spit you are not likely ever to roast a chicken as theory dictates that it should be done. In many parts of Europe a bird is roasted before an open flame or in front of coals. It is turned on a spit in such a manner as to preserve on the chicken most of the juices which it exudes. This is a wonderful way to cook a chicken, but is within the reach of relatively few families in this country. For most Americans, therefore, the term roast chicken means what is in actual fact an oven-baked chicken. This can be very good, especially if it is cooked in a slow oven and if the bird is filled with a good stuffing. Reliable timing schedules are printed in many cookbooks. We prefer a 325° oven.

THE IMPORTANCE OF STUFFING

There are many recipes for making stuffing. We use part of a loaf of French bread, sliced, as the base of the stuffing. The bread is, of course, little more than edible blotting paper. What gives the stuffing—and the bird—its flavor is the seasoning with which the bread is moistened. This calls for at least a cup of good stock or its equivalent. Into this should be put a large onion cut up in fine pieces. After the onion has cooked for about ten minutes in the stock, add three or four cut-up celery stalks and a diced carrot. Then comes the actual task of seasoning. If you have fresh herbs use at least a teaspoon apiece of chopped tarragon, chopped marjoram and chopped parsley, and a half teaspoon of chopped thyme. It is also worth putting in about a quarter teaspoon of chopped rosemary. If you do not have these fresh herbs use either dried herbs, or some of the herb seasoning powders such as those that the Spice Island Company puts up. You can also buy little packages especially designed to use in poultry stuffings. Better get a good brand, or you may be disappointed. In addition there should be at least a clove of garlic put through the garlic press, and as much salt and pepper as you like. If you are partial to spices try adding half a teaspoon of ginger and an eighth of a teaspoon of mace or allspice. Whatever the combinations used, the essential thing is that the broth should be strongly flavored, as it will be much diluted when it is mixed with the bread.

While the seasoned stock is cooking, shred enough bread so that when wet with the stock the volume will be about the size of the cavity of the bird. No precise rules can be given because of the difference in size of birds. A rough guide is to start with about twice as much bread (unmoistened) as you think will fit into the cavity. In other words, the bread will shrink at least half in volume when it is moistened. When the mixture is stuffed into the bird, the opening is sewed up. The making of stuffing is one of the few instances when it is well to be generous rather than cautious in seasoning. A good stuffing should have a pronounced flavor, in which herbs should predominate.

CHICKEN LEFTOVERS

Leftovers of chicken are useful. The two easiest and most obvious ways of using them are in a chicken salad and in the making of creamed chicken. One of the best chicken salads is the simplest—mix some mayonnaise with the cut-up bits of chicken.

If you plan to make creamed chicken use either chicken stock or one of the canned chicken broths in preparing the sauce in which the chicken is to be served. This will enhance the chicken flavor of the dish. Two or three finely sliced shallots cooked in the butter before the flour is added to make the *roux* will give the dish a distinctive flavor. Other seasonings that go well in a sauce for chicken are a touch of garlic, some cut-up tarragon leaves, soy sauce, or the remnants of the stuffing if you had a roasted bird and any remains. Dried or fresh mushrooms combine well with chicken. Cooked rice can also be added to a chicken sauce. If you plan to do this, and the rice was cooked a day or two before, it is well to boil it for two or three minutes in a small quantity of chicken stock. Be sure, however, that when you put this into the sauce you do not dilute the sauce too much. A still further variant is to place the chicken and its sauce, however seasoned, in a shallow baking dish, cover it with grated cheese and brown it under the broiler. The cheese adds a pleasant flavor to the dish.

CHICKEN STOCK

One of the advantages of a roast chicken is that you can nearly always get from a pint to a quart of chicken broth by breaking up and cooking the carcass and whatever remnants of meat you are not using in some other way. Suggestions for making this will be found in the chapter on soups. (See page 70.)

CHICKENS SOLD IN PIECES

In many communities there are shops in which you can buy portions of a chicken instead of having to get an entire bird. This is useful for small families or for individuals doing their own cooking. If you find such a store in your community, price wings and backs of chickens. If cheap—as often they are—you can use them for making a chicken stock in larger volume than would be possible if you had to rely only on the carcass and leftovers of a well-picked roasted chicken. Or try dishes which call for chicken livers. The livers are excellent in risottos, and are at their very best when sautéed for a scant two minutes in hot butter. If you overcook them they get tough.

TURKEYS NOW ARE SMALL

It is not necessary to go into the details of the preparation of a large turkey for Thanksgiving or Christmas dinner for a large family. But one of the most important developments of recent years in the poultry business is the breeding of streamlined small turkeys which run from about four to seven pounds apiece. We have found these birds not only excellent in taste but very useful. The reason for this is that one of these small roasters will serve from four to six people, with enough left over for several portions of cold turkey, creamed turkey or hash. Furthermore, the turkey carcass will yield a larger volume of broth than will a chicken of four to five pounds. It follows that when you buy one of these small birds you are likely to find that it goes farther than many other kinds of food.

The time schedule for cooking a turkey can be found in any cookbook. For stuffing it, follow the general suggestions given above for stuffing a roasting chicken. You will need about half again as much in quantity, as the cavity of the turkey is rather larger than that of a roasting chicken. If you like to stuff a turkey with oysters, or with bits of sausage, or with chestnuts, use any recipe which appeals to you—or combine some of these ingredients with the materials suggested for stuffing chicken. We like to serve with a turkey a gravy which is made by boiling the giblets for two to three hours in about two cups of water. When cooked this simmers down to about a cup or a cup and a half of good strong broth. With this broth a white sauce is made, and into this sauce the chopped giblets are put. The sauce will be the better for having a couple of tablespoons of thick cream added to it. It can then simmer—but not boil—until ready to serve.

For making creamed turkey follow the recipes above for creamed chicken. If you like a turkey hash you will find adequate recipes in some of the older cookbooks. It is usually a prosaic dish, but with imagination you can make it into something good. Incidentally, creamed turkey can be served by rolling it inside large pancakes about the size of a plate. The pancakes are then placed in a shallow oblong baking dish, and covered with some of the sauce in which the turkey has been creamed. Over this sprinkle a mild grated cheese, and place the dish under the broiler to brown. The baking dish should be hot when you put the pancakes with the turkey filling into it.

For making turkey broth follow the procedure outlined above for chicken broth.

DUCKS, DOMESTIC AND WILD

To lexicographers ducks are merely "lamellirostral natatorial birds"—i.e., birds which have flat beaks and swim. Yet for centuries gourmets from Peking to Paris have prized ducks as among the noblest of fowl. In the capital of imperial (and later of republican) China, duck dinners of many courses were tendered with pride to honored guests and eaten with relish by Chinese and foreigners. Duck soup, duck livers, breasts of duck variously prepared, and almost everything but the bills and feathers, were cooked with delicacy by some of the world's greatest culinary artists. In France, for a century or more, pressed duck has been a specialty of several of the most famous and expensive restaurants, such as the Tour d'Argent in Paris. In England the raising of Aylesbury ducks has long been profitable. On parts of the South Shore of Long Island, duck runs compete with commuters and vacationists for the few remaining unpre-empted feet of water front along the Great South Bay. Each autumn millions of duck hunters throughout the world look forward to rising before a cold gray dawn, and taking refuge in a well-camouflaged (and well-provisioned) blind, there to wait, shotgun in hand, till a flight of ducks presents itself for slaughter.

In the United States during this season conservationists write letters to the newspapers deploring the depletion of the duck population. Many of the writers, incidentally, secretly hope that a duck-hunting friend will remember them if the limit of his bag is not already bespoken.

Yet there is much controversy about ducks. Hunters, duck farmers, chefs and gourmets disagree about which kind are the best flavored, how they should be killed, how long to hang them, how to clean and pluck them, how to cook them and what to serve with them. The merits of Rouen, Aylesbury, Peking and Long Island ducks are upheld by their partisans. Among wild ducks mallards rank high, although some like sprig or ruddy duck. The French spurn ducks that have not been strangled. Some cooks say that no duck should ever be basted; others that a cup of red wine is a must in the basting liquid. There are disputes as to whether apples, onions, celery or slices of orange should be placed in the duck's cavity during the cooking. On two things only do duck hunters agree—that wild ducks should be hung till high, and that they should be cooked so briefly that the meat is red and runny.

On the few but welcome occasions when a neighbor has given us wild ducks which he has shot we have followed two simple rules: First, we have asked when the hunter advises eating them, and then have served them two days earlier. Second, we have asked his advice on how long to cook them, and in how hot an oven, and then have doubled the time and reduced the heat by 10 per cent. We usually put cut-up celery and onion in the bird's cavity. Our timing, based on considerable experimenting, is about forty minutes in a 400° oven. As this, from the hunter's point of view, is heresy, desecration and ingratitude rolled into one, we keep this fact secret. But to non-hunters we can bear witness that ducks thus cooked are delectable. If the birds are not plump, strips of bacon may be laid over the breasts. The resulting fat should be used for basting.

If you live near sources of domestic ducks try any recipe which appeals to you, but bear in mind that duck fat, like the fat of geese, is cloying, and should be used with discretion and in only very small amounts. Like most birds, the more often a duck is basted the better the end product will be. And don't overlook the liver. It is a pity to waste its fine flavor in a sauce or stuffing. Try sautéing it in butter. As it is larger than chicken liver, it should be cooked a little longer. Two minutes on each side usually is enough, unless it is exceptionally large. Overcooking will make it tough.

Sprinkle it with salt and a bit of fresh-ground pepper, and serve on toast over which the butter in which it was cooked is poured. It goes well with a drink while the rest of the meal is finishing cooking. You are likely to seek out a "repeat performance" and thereafter to keep a weather eye for domestic ducks when in the market. Incidentally, another merit of the domestic duck is that the carcass (especially if the bird has been oven roasted) makes a soup which amply justifies the implication of the slang expression. Follow the suggestions for making chicken or turkey soup. If the bones can be cracked or broken so much the better. When simmered for three or four hours treat it as you would chicken stock. Better use very little of the fat if you plan to thicken the soup with a *roux*, until, by tasting, you know the flavor which it will impart. Butter is the best substitute. Or, if you like the duck-fat flavor, a mixture of butter and fat. Recommended seasonings: lemon juice, garlic, monosodium glutamate, powdered ginger (all in small quantities) and soy sauce (to taste).

SQUABS—FOR BIG MONEY

One bird remains to be considered—squab. Unfortunately this is a very expensive dish. I say "unfortunately" because it is one of the finest of all foods.

The best way to cook a squab is to split or halve it, and grill it over charcoal. If you cannot do this, try grilling it under a broiler, but be sure to baste it so that it does not get too dry. Also be sure not to overcook it. Squabs should be eaten while still juicy. They can be on the reddish side. No fancier way of cooking a squab brings out the flavor as well as this simple old recipe.

MANY MEN'S MEAT 9

Much meat is tough. But the writing of a chapter about meat is tougher. The reason for this is that tender cuts of meat are expensive and generally are used sparingly. Furthermore, meats vary in utility according to the number of persons to be fed. For example, a three- or four-rib roast of beef, a four- to six-pound leg of lamb, or half a ham will furnish many servings. Yet recent figures in the *Statistical Abstract of the United States* show that approximately four out of every five families in these United States number four persons or less, and three out of five families comprise only three persons or less. What this means in terms of housekeeping is that a large proportion of housewives in the United States face the problem of how to cook for few, rather than for many, persons.

COOKING FOR FEW

This makes the choice of meats hard. There are, of course, cuts which are not too large for two to four persons. These include some of the relatively cheaper meats. It is also easy to buy steak for a small family—at a price. Lamb chops are usually available—also at a price. Often you can buy calf's liver, which can be tastefully prepared and is supposed to be health-giving. But this also is costly. The other so-called internal organs, such as kidneys, sweetbreads and brains, are relatively unpopular, but lend themselves well to cooking for a small number of people, even though they take long to prepare.

There is a further complication—that so many cuts of meat which can be bought in small amounts and at reasonable prices are hard to prepare attractively. Boiled meat of almost any kind is less palatable than roast, broiled, grilled or even fried meat. This is why the word "stew" has never had a good connotation among Americans. The French produce excellent dishes much like stews, but under more attractive names. These are improved by skillfully disguising—or rather, amplifying—the flavor of the meat used. Such cookery is hard to master.

KINDS OF MEAT

In cookbook usage the term "meat" covers beef, veal, lamb and mutton, and pork. Venison is classed as "game." It is, in fact, the only meat occasionally sold under that classification in the United States, with the exception of rabbit. It was not so, however, in our grandparents' day. Mr. Blot, to whose cookbook of ninety years ago I have several times referred, extols bear meat and buffalo. Of the former he says that it has a "highly nutritive quality and is very warming." He advises broiling buffalo meat directly on the coals without a gridiron, and using wood ashes instead of salt by way of seasoning. This was the Plains Indians' custom when herds of buffalo thundered across the unfenced prairies of the Middle West a century ago. Mr. Blot also includes directions for the cooking of opossum, otter, raccoon, skunk, fox and woodchuck, and has a special paragraph about how to skin a skunk. This last skill would seem to be a somewhat superfluous and outdated branch of knowledge for modern American apartment dwellers—

Many Men's Meat

unless, of course, it could be applied to humans of that species.

Bears, possums and coons and other game animals are still eaten in parts of the United States—doubtless a culinary heritage of frontier days. On a hunting trip with Theodore Roosevelt in northern Arizona in the summer of 1913 I ate—and enjoyed—mountain lion meat, which tastes much like the venison on which most cougars dine. An old-timer who lives in a remote canyon a few miles from us on the California coast assures me that the meat of the wildcat is excellent, and reports that the Chinese in Monterey pay him well for a wildcat, which, when cooked according to a special Chinese recipe, is reputed to make Chinese men more attractive to Chinese ladies, and vice versa. The basis of the recipe consists in stewing the wildcat in whiskey with sugar cane, ginseng, salt, and several herbs imported from China. One of these is known as *tung-ch'ung-ts'ao,* which, being translated, means "winter worm herb." Another is *lung-yen-kan-jou,* which means "dried meat of the fruit of the dragon's eye." As I have not tasted this wildcat stew I cannot vouch for its efficacy, but I doubt that it is as cataclysmic as the potion which Brangaene gave Isolde in Wagner's opera *Tristan.* As the Chinese herbs are hard to find, and wildcats are scarce outside of oil fields, few readers of this book are likely to attempt this recipe.

GRILLING OVER CHARCOAL

Let us begin by considering briefly meats which lend themselves to one or another method of cooking. If you have a charcoal grill you will wish to cook steaks on it. There is no better way of doing a steak—including the system devised for a French king, in which a *filet mignon* was cooked between two thinner cuts which were discarded when the fillet was finished. Many articles and even books have been written about what some like to term the "art" of barbecuing. It would perhaps be more accurate to call this a form of culinary exhibitionism. A true barbecue centers about the cooking and serving of an entire animal—usually a cow or sheep, sometimes a hog. But except on rare, festive occasions in the West—particularly in California, Texas and parts of the cow country—it is practically never used as a method of preparing meat.

In modern America the term "barbecuing" is usually applied to the singeing of steaks over a too hot fire by a host who wears a chef's hat to show that he is master of his newly acquired avocation. Even those who have learned how to barbecue steaks well usually feel obliged to douse the steaks in pungent sauces and seasonings, which often overwhelm the natural flavor of the meat. Others insist on rubbing the meat with garlic, or drenching it in soy sauce, or marinating it in vinegar and oil. This is all right for a change. But before doing this try cooking whatever cut of steak you like in the simplest possible manner: grease the grill so that the meat will not stick and, after wiping the meat with a damp cloth and drying it a bit, place it on the grill over the charcoal after the fire has stopped smoking, without salt or any kind of seasoning. Incidentally, cut off any fat that the butcher has left on it, as this will otherwise drip on the charcoal and make it flame, which tends to spoil the fine flavor of the steak. At the end of about three minutes turn the steak and salt the side that has just browned. When another three minutes have passed, turn it again, and salt the other side. Thereafter continue turning it every two or three minutes until it is done. In this manner it will cook through. Tastes differ as to how a steak should be served. Most gourmets are inclined to agree that it should be rare, rather than overdone. It is difficult to give an arbitrary time schedule, as two variables are involved—the thickness of the steak and the heat of the fire. The thinner the steak and the hotter the fire the shorter will be the cooking time. We find that a steak of about an inch to an inch and a quarter thick takes from ten to fourteen minutes.

Steak is not the only meat which lends itself well to grilling over charcoal. If your butcher is friendly, get him to bone a shoulder of lamb and cut out as much of the fat and gristle as possible. This will give you a rather chunky looking mass of meat, usually in several pieces and of different thicknesses and shapes. The chances are that no matter how willing he is to help you he will leave in the meat more fat and gristle than is desirable if it is to be grilled. It is well, therefore, to go over it with a sharp knife and cut out the fat which he has left. The meat then is treated just like a steak. Do not be disturbed by the fact that some of the chunks will be thinner than others. Watch the thin ones lest they cook too much. The rare parts of lamb cooked in this manner are as good as are the overdone parts which have become charred from the heat and occasional smoke from the drippings. This is an admirable and always popular grilled-meat dish.

BROILING BY GAS OR ELECTRICITY

If you use a broiler in a gas or electric stove the same caution should be heeded in cooking a steak as in broiling a chicken—beware lest it dry too much. One way to check this is to leave the door to the unit partly open. This discourages the accumulation of intense heat, and thus prevents the juices of the meat from being sucked out. Stoves are not uniform in their reactions. Try basting with butter if the meat seems to be drying too much.

ROASTING MEANS BAKING

Roasting, as has been indicated in the previous chapter, should really be called baking. It is simple, and has the advantage of requiring little attention. The main principles are:

1. Take the meat out of the refrigerator long enough ahead of the hour when it is to be put in the oven so that it will have acquired room temperature. The larger the piece of meat, the longer this will take.

2. Avoid using a hot oven, as excessive heat reduces the volume and dries up the juices of the meat. It is best to put roasts in an oven not hotter than 325°. We have experimented with much lower heats, and have had some interesting and promising results, but the techniques of very slow cooking—say in an oven of 180° to 200°—have not been sufficiently tested to be definitive. Over against the advice to use a slow oven is the testimony of some of the masters of roasting who

insist that you should, to begin with, put the meat to be roasted in a very hot oven—say from 400° to 425° —for a half hour, reducing the heat thereafter. Some day it may be possible to prove scientifically and gustatorially which system is better. We have always had good results using a 325° oven throughout.

3. Avoid strong seasoning, except in the case of lamb, which is the better for being rubbed generously with crushed garlic before being salted. Do not make slits and insert cloves of garlic, even though this is recommended by good French cooks. If you do, the meat will "bleed" and lose its juices.

4. By all means baste frequently, beginning about three-quarters of an hour after the meat has been put in the oven. The operation should be repeated about every ten to fifteen minutes. Within the last few years makers of heat-proof glassware have put out a gadget which is referred to in our kitchen as "the little bastard." It is like a big eye dropper, made of Pyrex glass which will stand the heat of hot fat. Incidentally, if a cut of meat is slow in rendering its fat, use a couple of tablespoons of whatever cooking fat you have on hand —preferably a bland vegetable oil rather than butter or olive oil. The former burns too easily. The latter is too strong.

Many Men's Meat

As roast meat should not be overcooked it is wise to plan your time schedule so that the roast will not be ready until from fifteen to thirty minutes after the guests are expected to arrive. In the event that they have not come within fifteen minutes before the roast should be ready, and if you plan to serve cocktails, turn the oven down to its lowest point. This will prevent overcooking, yet keep the roast warm.

You will find timing schedules in standard books of recipes. We figure seventeen minutes per pound in a 325° over for rare roast beef, and twenty-five minutes per pound for a leg of lamb.

PAN FRYING

Few meats other than pork chops are fried with creditable results. The exception to this is a thin slice of beef or of venison which can be cooked in a very hot pan in which a small amount of fat has been placed. This is called "pan frying," and is used for the cooking of a minute steak, which, incidentally, can be an excellent dish if the meat is good and the pan is of the right heat. We have successfully substituted salt for fat in the pan (and, of course, have then omitted salting the meat). The salt prevents the meat from sticking to the pan.

In my youth, as I said in the foreword, we thought that steaks fried in bacon grease marked the summit of culinary achievement. Incidentally, we also thought that potatoes baked in the ashes of a campfire until they were charred stood next to steak at the top of the list of food for angels—and boys. If there were no other way of doing steaks and potatoes nowadays I would make the most of them. But one of the compensations of advancing years is the realization that experience in almost any field is likely to change one's standards of values. When, a few years ago, I tried frying a steak in bacon fat I regretted that I had not grilled the steak, or broiled it. Why spoil the rich and delicate flavor of a good cut of beef by drenching it in the coarse, strong taste of the average bacon grease?

STEWS BY ANY OTHER NAME

There remains the problem—and, as I have said on page 120, it is one of the most difficult problems which any cook has to face—of cooking meats in some sort of liquid. Experts distinguish between at least four ways of so doing. The first is braising, in which meat is cooked in a small amount of liquid in a closely covered pan. The next is steam roasting, in which an even smaller quantity of liquid is used in a covered roasting

Many Men's Meat

pan, and in which the meat is cooked by action of the steam generated. The third is simmering, which, as the name indicates, means the cooking of meat at a temperature just under boiling. The fourth, and, fortunately, the most rarely used, is straight boiling, by which is meant covering the meat with liquid and cooking it on top of the stove at a moderate to strong boil. This is a sure way to ruin good meat.

All these processes lead to the same thing—in simplest English, to some kind of stew. The cooking is necessarily slow, as only so can the tougher cuts of meat be made tender. The taste of many of these tougher cuts is good. The problem is how to retain some, at least, of the agreeable flavor in the meat itself, and not to have the meat be like a spent sponge. The usual French manner of solving this problem is to lard the meat before cooking it. The process is not easy for amateurs, but if your butcher is not too busy, ask him to lard the meat for you. He will do this with strips of the fat of salt pork. The purpose of larding is to distribute fat throughout a piece of meat which is lacking in fat of its own.

There are several points of kinship in these various ways of cooking meat in liquids. The first is that, whether or not the meat has been larded, it is usually floured and browned in hot fat before being placed in the cooking pot with the liquid. The next is that the extracts exuded by the meat in the process of cooking, however good they may be unadorned, almost always are reinforced by the addition of vegetables, herbs, wine, stock or some other form of seasoning. There are countless recipes for pot roasts, ragouts, daubes, stews, goulashes and other similar meat dishes, whatever the name of the dish and the country of its origin. The fact that so many of these recipes call for onion and many also for garlic, to be put in from the start of the stewing, braising or pot roasting, suggests that this is a must. Among herbs, marjoram, thyme and rosemary deserve attention. Be cautious in using bay in any kind of stew or cooked-meat dish as the flavor is pervasive and almost impossible to modify or eradicate. Also be careful with salt. If meat is salted freely the liquid in which the meat has been cooked may, when it is boiled down, become so salty as to be almost unusable. This would deprive you of one of the most valuable by-products of the pot roasting, braising or stewing processes.

THE USEFUL CASSEROLE

Many dishes which come under the foregoing heads can be prepared in casserole pots which can be brought to the table for serving. This is a distinct advance in modern cooking and eating habits. If you can manage to have casserole dishes of different sizes you will find them handy, as the more closely a piece of meat fits into the pot in which it is to be stewed, braised or pot roasted, the less liquid it will need and the richer and more concentrated will be the juice which will come out of it. Meats cooked in this way should be turned several times so as to prevent any part from drying out.

If you will glance over various cookbooks you will see that the combinations of vegetables to be cooked with meats in casseroles or other covered containers are almost limitless. The lesson of this is: make your own selection, and experiment.

MEAT LOAVES

Meat loaves made with imagination and care can be very good. The base is about two or three parts of ground beef or veal to one of pork. But the seasoning is preserved and transmitted through bread or bread crumbs soaked in highly flavored liquid. We make ours by cooking about a half cup each of cut-up onion, celery and carrots in a scant cup of stock, seasoned with garlic and herbs, a bit of Worcestershire and lemon, to which, when the vegetables are cooked, is added a tablespoon of brandy. The seasoning should be rather sharp. The stock and vegetables are mixed with about two cups of shredded bread, and this in turn is thoroughly worked into the combined meats. They will probably need some extra salt and fresh-ground pepper. A beaten egg is then stirred in, and the whole put in a well-greased baking dish in a 325° oven. If it tends to dry, baste it with a few spoons of heated red wine. Cooking time—a minimum of an hour and a quarter.

MEAT RESERVES

If your meal planning is often upset by unexpected changes in numbers, and you do not live near a market, you may want to keep on hand a few frozen meats and also some cans of corned beef, corned-beef hash and roast-beef hash. Corned beef can be made into an excellent hash by adding potato, onion and bits of cut-up bacon. The last two need only a small amount of seasoning, such as some Worcestershire, grated onion and, perhaps, a drop or two of the juice of crushed garlic. We have found that one of the advantages of a ham bought in the market and cooked at home is that it keeps long, and can be used in many ways to please unexpected guests. A boiled tongue, while lacking a ham's long-keeping advantages, also lends itself to extra servings, either cold or hot. It is a good addition to a platter of cold cuts. So are some of the large precooked sausages of the salami or bologna type.

Unfortunately most of these are coarse in flavor. In fact, in no branch of meat marketing have the American packers produced so much inferior stuff as in the preparing and marketing of sausages of all kinds. This, which still is an art in Europe, has been bastardized, commercialized and standardized in the United States to such an extent that the public's taste, always docile, has become dulled. Even the supposedly highest-class "farm" sausages are so dominated by strong and inferior fats that it is virtually impossible to prepare them so that they resemble the old-fashioned homemade sausages of this country, or any of the better sausages made in Europe. A really good sausage can be a dish for epicures. Rarely is such a dish available in the United States. In the light of the enormous production and consumption of pork products in this country this is a sorry reflection on the lack of imagination of the meat packers. Surely one of them should find it good business to market really high-grade sausage meat, or to can, deep freeze or otherwise prepare for long-range use sausages that have a minimum of fat, and that are well seasoned by experts. We were served such sausages, homemade, at a little restaurant in Nephi, Utah, eighteen years ago, and still remember them with pleasure—and with regret that we have never found their equals.

VARIED 10
VEGETABLES

Vegetables may be considered under three heads: (1) fresh and frozen; (2) canned; and (3) dried.

FRESH AND FROZEN VEGETABLES

Fresh and frozen vegetables are lumped together because the ways of cooking them are much the same. Fresh vegetables are, of course, preferable, if you can get them truly fresh. There is no substitute for your own vegetable garden—not even the garden of a generous friend. But as between so-called fresh vegetables that have been lying around for several days in a market, or on the way to market, and frozen vegetables which have been properly put up, the latter are likely to be better. Frozen vegetables have the further advantage of coming prepared, not even needing washing. The saving of time and work is substantial. The main difference between frozen and fresh vegetables is that, excellent as are so many of the frozen vegetables, they are likely to lack the full delicacy of flavor of the really fresh article. It follows, therefore, that you may wish to experiment in giving a little more seasoning to frozen vegetables of the kind described in the following paragraphs as having delicate flavors. Doubtless, as the quick-freezing process is further perfected, the minor differences between fresh and frozen foods will become even less perceptible. Already they are small. Incidentally, don't keep frozen vegetables longer than a single season, despite the fact that the makers of deep-freeze units list the approximate storage period of all vegetables except asparagus and stewed tomatoes as from eight to twelve months. The last two should be used early.

Fresh and frozen vegetables may be subdivided into three groups: (1) those that have a delicate flavor; (2) those whose flavor is coarse; and (3) the group in between whose flavor is not pronounced. The reason for dividing them this way is that the delicacy, coarse-

Varied Vegetables

ness or mildness of flavor of a particular vegetable is an indication of how this vegetable should be prepared.

Delicate Vegetables

For example, among the delicate-flavored vegetables (I am here speaking only of fresh or frozen vegetables, not of canned vegetables) are young peas, young string beans and limas, young carrots and beets, young corn, mushrooms, asparagus and artichokes. Practically all of these are at their best served with no other seasoning than the salt in the water in which they were cooked, and a bit of butter poured over them. It is true that asparagus is excellent with a hollandaise or other more elaborate sauce, and that artichokes can be prepared in many tasty ways which call for the use of such strong seasonings even as garlic. Yet if these vegetables are at their freshest, and are truly young, they are so savory that it is a pity to overwhelm them with stronger flavors.

Fresh corn, young and not picked too long, will nearly always be adequately cooked if you drop the ears in boiling salted water and as soon as the water begins to boil again, remove them. This process usually takes only three or four minutes. The less time between the picking and the cooking of corn the better it will taste. This, however, is not a matter over which many housewives can exercise control. The ideal procedure is to pick corn in your own garden not longer than fifteen minutes before you expect to serve it.

Corn lends itself to the making of an excellent old-fashioned corn pudding. We use a family recipe which dates from my great-grandmother's day, and which calls for ears of ripe corn, which are grated. The process is slow and tiring. When you are through with the grater, scrape the cobs with a kitchen knife so as to transfer as much as possible of the remaining milk and pulp into the dish. When you have grated whatever quantity you plan to make—you will need at least four ears per portion (and preferably six)—mix into the corn a generous quantity of butter—at least three tablespoons per cup of grated corn. Add plenty of salt, as corn eats it up, pour the entire mixture into a well-greased baking dish and put it in a 325° oven. It will take from forty-five minutes to an hour to cook it properly. Please note that no milk or cream or eggs or any kind of seasoning other than butter and salt go into this dish. If you try it with good corn—and be sure that it is well ripened—you will want a repeat

Varied Vegetables

performance, despite the work involved in grating and scraping the corn. It is the best of all corn dishes.

An easier but often neglected way to cook corn is to remove the silk, but not the husks, from ears of corn, and, after holding them under the tap so as to get as much water as possible into the husks, place the ears in a 325° oven for about twenty to twenty-five minutes. We usually take the ears out of the husks before serving them. This is a matter of taste. Incidentally, should you be grilling a steak or chicken, and have room on the grill, place corn in the husks over the charcoal beside the meat. The corn will have a fine nutty flavor. It is cooked when the husks begin to turn brown or burn.

Coarse Vegetables

Strong or coarse-flavored vegetables need careful preparation. Among the coarser vegetables are all the members of the cabbage tribe—cabbage, cauliflower, kohlrabi, Brussels sprouts, broccoli and kale—as well as turnips and most of the members of the onion tribe.

It is particularly important not to overcook these vegetables. Cooks of British or north European origin or descent long insisted that cabbage must be boiled for from twenty to forty minutes and that cauliflower also should be long cooked. Today most cooks know better, and most cookbooks have shortened the recommended cooking time. Cabbage can be made even more tasty if the cooking time is cut below that recommended in cookbooks. We shred a cabbage to be cooked—using preferably a reasonably small green cabbage—as if it were being prepared for cole slaw. It is then put into a large pot full of salted boiling water, and the moment the water recovers the boil, the cabbage is removed and strained and is ready to serve with the addition of a generous amount of butter. It is crisp, has a good taste and lacks the strong, sulphurous flavor characteristic of the overboiled cabbages so dear to the palates of the English, Irish and Germans—and most of the inhabitants of the northern United States and Canada.

Cauliflower also is better when not cooked too long. The exact time depends on the size and age of the head, and the number of days since it was picked. One of the best ways of preparing a cauliflower for further treatment is to steam it, rather than to boil it. However cooked, a cauliflower gains by the addition of modifying sauces, such as a cream sauce, or a cheese sauce (see page 54), or a hollandaise. An excellent way of serving cauliflower is with a polonaise sauce, which is

Varied Vegetables

made by adding bread crumbs to browned butter and cooking them briefly, until they stop frothing. Lemon juice is then added. The sauce is poured over the cauliflower and over all is spread chopped parsley and finely chopped hard-boiled eggs.

Broccoli, if very fresh, and if cooked in little water for the minimum amount of time to make the stems tender, can be excellent when served with a hollandaise sauce. No rule for timing can be given, as everything depends on the freshness of the particular bunch of broccoli which you are cooking.

Brussels sprouts presumably can be made palatable. The indomitable English have eaten the vegetable for centuries, despite the fact that British cooks have never managed to devise a means of ridding it of its concentrated essence of all that is strongest, most pertinacious and most sulphurous in the entire cabbage family. Clearly, there is no accounting for tastes.

The usual way of cooking onions in the United States is to fry or boil them. If the particular kind of onion is not too strong and if the fat in which the onions are fried is fresh and not too heavy, this dish is deservedly popular. Even better is to do them in the so-called French style, in which the onion slices or rings are dipped in milk and flour, or in a batter, and then cooked in deep fat. The disadvantage of this process is that it is fairly slow. If you have good deep-frying equipment—that is to say, a metal basket which fits into a pan, or an electrically operated heater, which is deep enough to hold the oil or fat in which you are going to do the frying—it is worth the time and effort.

Boiled onions are good when served in a white sauce which not only has a fair amount of lemon in it to counteract the excessive sweetness of the onions, but also enough other seasoning to make it savory. The best onions for boiling are small and as young as possible. A pinch of sugar in the water in which the onions are cooked is reputed to cut the sharpness of the onion flavor.

In parts of Europe onions are also oven cooked, like baked potatoes. The outer skin is then removed. Only the inside is eaten, with the addition of butter and salt. The cooking time depends on the size of the onions and the heat of the oven. In France the usual custom is to place them in a roasting pan in what they call a hot oven—which without more definite information I would imagine would be in an oven of about 400°. Medium-sized onions cooked this way should take an hour or a little more.

Onions vary in strength. Consult your grocer or

Varied Vegetables

vegetable dealer. The so-called Bermuda and Spanish onions are among the milder, and, within reason, can be used raw without obliterating all other flavors.

Mild Vegetables

Tomatoes and celery are at their best when various things are done to them in the cooking and seasoning. Tomatoes in the United States traditionally are just plain boiled. It is all right to serve canned tomatoes this way—provided you will do them the honor of adding onion, herbs and a fair amount of seasoning. But there are better ways of making tomatoes attractive listed in various cookbooks. We are partial to a simple way of broiling them in which, besides a little salt and fresh-ground pepper and monosodium glutamate, only butter and bread crumbs are put on them before they are placed under the broiler. If you like the flavor of tarragon and have some handy, sprinkle chopped tarragon leaves on the tomatoes before adding the butter and bread crumbs. The tomatoes should be halved.

Cooked celery is nearest its pure state when it is braised, as is so often done in France. In that country, celery, split and cut lengthwise, is usually blanched in boiling water before being put in a covered baking dish with butter and allowed to cook slowly until tender. Some of the French like to add a little soup stock or meat glaze in the process. It is sure to enhance the flavor. The other popular way of doing celery is to cut it up in medium-sized pieces and cook it in a small volume of water. Use the cooking water with a little white *roux* to make a sauce for the celery. Cream may be added.

Among the other milder vegetables are potatoes, yams and sweet potatoes, zucchini, parsnips, spinach, salsify, squashes and that strange and tasteless gourd so popular in England under the name of vegetable marrow.

Pepping Up Potatoes

Potatoes, which can be so good, too often are prepared in a spirit of resignation rather than of gustatory anticipation. This may be because they are easy to bake and boil. Unfortunately the boiling process, which is preparatory to the making of various potato dishes, is often poorly carried out. Either the potatoes are not thoroughly cooked or they are overdone. A safe way is to start them in cold water in their jackets, and cook them by feel rather than by rule—that is, until they spear easily with a fork. Yet even at their best, boiled

Varied Vegetables

potatoes cry out for special seasoning. I know of no better way to do this than to mix chopped fresh herbs in butter to be poured over the potatoes. Chives and parsley are indicated. In addition, try any other herbs you happen to like or have on hand. We use marjoram, thyme, tarragon or basil.

These herbs added to mashed potatoes transform the dish into a delight. Incidentally, the milk which usually is added to mashed potatoes furnishes a good vehicle for carrying into the potatoes almost any kind of flavoring that you may like. Try grating a quarter of an onion into it, or putting in a little Worcestershire, or a drop of garlic, or almost any kind of seasoning that appeals to you. Should you be so fortunate as to grow or to find in the market some young new potatoes —the size of a golf ball or smaller—try parboiling them for a few minutes and then sautéing them in butter in which you have chopped up a little rosemary.

Baked potatoes are deservedly popular. You will win friends for your cooking skill if you not only oil the potatoes thoroughly with olive oil but put on them a generous amount of salt before cooking them. They require about an hour in a hot oven, depending, of course, on their size and freshness. They should be pierced with a fork before cooking. The newer-harvested potatoes take longer to cook than do those which have been long stored.

Yams and Sweets

Yams and sweet potatoes are said by nutritionists to be richer in vitamins and essential minerals than the ordinary white potato. Whether or not this is true, these tubers are too little used north of the Mason and Dixon line. Not only are they good when baked in their skins just as is a white potato, but they lend themselves to at least two distinctly festive dishes. The first is the traditional candied yams or sweets which accompany the Christmas or Thanksgiving meal. You will find recipes for this in most cookbooks. The second is a sweet potato or yam soufflé. The principle ingredients in this, besides the mashed tubers, which have been previously boiled, are a substantial amount of butter together with perhaps as much as a half teaspoon each of ginger, allspice and cinnamon. We also add a half cup of rum. When all of this has been thoroughly mixed, beat separately the yolks and whites of four eggs. Mix in the yolks thoroughly, and fold in the whites. Place the dish in a 375° oven until the top and sides are well browned. This should take about thirty minutes. Allow about a half cup of potato per person.

Varied Vegetables

A final word on the cooking of vegetables, whether fresh or frozen. Whenever possible cook them in a pan with a heavy bottom. Do not use high heat. For almost all vegetables with the exception of corn and members of the cabbage tribe, use the smallest possible amount of water. If you are afraid that they may scorch, add a tablespoon of butter at the end of the first five or six minutes. Remember that it is better to undercook rather than to overcook vegetables. Except on rare occasions when tomatoes happen to be excessively bitter and acid, never use soda in cooking vegetables.

CANNED VEGETABLES

There are many canned vegetables. For decades they made vegetables available regardless of the growing season, and saved time in the preparation of meals. But unless the canners show unaccustomed ingenuity in improving the quality of their wares they will lose to the processors of frozen foods. Most canned vegetables are purely utilitarian in value. They keep long, and are useful in emergencies. But it is hard to dress them up so as to make them attractive to persons who enjoy good food.

There are, of course, some notable exceptions. Canned tomatoes, as already indicated, can be used almost interchangeably with fresh tomatoes except for grilling and for salads. We have found excellent canned French-fried onions, and good small white onions. Canned corn, while different from fresh corn, can be made into good dishes. The same, unfortunately, is untrue of canned green beans, and of almost all canned peas with the possible exception of a few of the French varieties. We have found the canned so-called "extra small" whole beets good in salads or served as a hot vegetable. For either use we discard the liquid in which the beets are put up.

DRIED LEGUMES

Before the days of canning—which is to say, before the middle of the last century—dried vegetables not only were esteemed but had the added value of keeping from season to season. Most households laid in stocks of dried beans, peas or lentils for winter eating. The custom dates back to remote antiquity, and originated independently in various parts of the world. The variety of dried vegetables differed in different areas—from the soybeans of northeast Asia to the limas of South America, and from the white beans of the Mediterranean region to the red kidney and pinto beans of North America. Archaeologists have found evidences

Varied Vegetables

that beans and lentils were eaten in the Bronze Age in Europe, and have unearthed lima beans with mummies in Peru.

In American households today dried legumes are too little used, despite the fact that most of them can be quickly and easily cooked in a pressure cooker. Many persons who might otherwise use them are deterred by the universal recommendation in American cookbooks that they be soaked for twelve hours, more or less, before cooking. The great Escoffier, on the other hand, insists that they should never be soaked. With commendable impartiality the booklets put out by some of the pressure-cooker makers give the cooking time for unsoaked as well as for soaked dried legumes. Thus, obviously, you can take your choice.

The most famous of American dried-bean dishes—Boston baked beans—is a good cranny-filler. New Englanders satisfy their sense of the nostalgic—as well as give proof of their lack of imagination—by eating the same old bean-pot dish fifty-two weeks a year from the cradle to the grave, taking pride in never departing a tittle from the recipe handed down from Great-Aunt Sarah's grandmother whose husband was killed at Bunker Hill. To some this will seem to be a mark of veneration for custom and tradition rather than of gustatorial discrimination. As one who is a quarter New Englander by descent, I would not attempt to question the New Englanders' notion of what they think is right. But I should like to see a competition held to judge the relative merits of Boston baked beans, a cassoulet from the south of France and a dish of frijoles prepared by a good Mexican cook, in all of which dishes dried beans are a main ingredient. I would gladly bet that I could pick the loser.

As a cassoulet calls for the rather delicate white beans of France, and must have bits of goose and other items difficult to get in these United States, it is rarely served here. But an imaginative chef can use recipes for making a cassoulet de Toulouse or à la Castelnaudary and, by substituting items available in this country, can create a bean dish which any gourmet would relish.

Easier to make are the variations of Mexican beans. Preferences differ as to the variety of bean to use. We happen to like the red kidney. Others like the pinto. Follow your favorite recipe, but go light on the Mexican peppers. For fat try lard rather than any of the vegetable oils. Be generous with garlic, and use a teaspoon of chopped oregano. Some cooks like to cook a ham bone with the beans. Others put in cubes of salt pork or bacon. The essential point is that there must be a generous amount of fat, and that this should preferably have originated on a porker. Besides this, beans are the better for strong seasonings.

Boiled dried beans can be used as a pleasant alternative to roast potatoes accompanying a leg of lamb. Put them in the roasting pan about forty-five minutes before the roast is done, and baste them frequently. If there is an excessive amount of fat in the pan, skim off part of it before putting in the beans, so that they do not become too greasy. An excess of lamb fat, like mutton tallow, has an unpleasant flavor and quality.

Lentils, either plain boiled, or puréed, make a good accompaniment to sausages. Try adding two tablespoons of olive oil, a clove of garlic and a quarter of an onion, grated, to the lentils as they cook. They take only about fifteen minutes in a pressure cooker.

It is to be hoped that dried soybeans will become increasingly available. Nutritionists describe them as one of the most nourishing of all legumes. To date they are scarcely mentioned in books of recipes, and can usually be bought only in "health food" stores. Keep an eye out for them, and for promising recipes which call for their use.

SOME SO-CALLED 11 STARCHES

Americans have become increasingly pasta-conscious in recent years. They enjoy macaroni and spaghetti in many forms, as well as their close kin, noodles. For this they owe thanks to Italian immigrants and their descendents.

THE USEFUL PASTAS

Excellent one-dish meals can be made with one of the pastas, as can a main course of a good lunch or supper. Pastas take kindly to seasoning, being bland by nature. Their chief drawback is that they are fattening, not only because of the flour in them but because

Some So-Called Starches

so many of the sauces served with them are rich in butter or olive oil.

PASTAS SHOULD NOT BE OVERCOOKED

The cooking of any of the pastas calls, in the first place, for a kettle large enough to hold plenty of hard-boiling, well-salted water. As they should not be overcooked, and as pastas of the same type differ in cooking time when put up by different makers, it is wise to test a pasta after it has boiled for ten minutes. Most of them take longer. To be sure, experiment to see just how long the kind you use takes in your own kitchen.

Because fully cooked pastas do not keep well—they tend to get sticky and chunky—pastas should be started at the latest possible moment before being eaten. In some restaurants they are precooked until within two or three minutes of being done. They are then removed, washed thoroughly and put aside until called for, when they are placed in a strainer or colander and returned to a kettle of strongly boiling water until the cooking is completed and the pasta is cooked but still firm. I have not tried this system, but see no reason why it should not be adaptable to home cooking.

SEASONING THE PASTAS

One of the simplest and best ways to season pasta is to melt a substantial amount of butter—the quantity depends on the volume of pasta to be served—in which two cloves of crushed garlic are lightly cooked for a couple of minutes. If you have a good olive oil you may prefer to use the oil instead of the butter as a vehicle to disseminate the flavor of the garlic. Another standard way of making a sauce for a pasta is to use tomatoes in one or other form—fresh, canned solid pack, tomato paste or tomato sauce. Tomatoes have a special affinity for the pastas. They should be cooked in butter or oil and reasonably highly seasoned with fresh-ground pepper and any herbs which you happen to like. Both basil and oregano are indicated. For a more elaborate sauce the Italians add ground beef or pork, and also grated or thinly sliced onions which are cooked in the butter or oil before the tomatoes are added. Another good sauce is made by adding crushed anchovies to the butter or oil. One of our special favorites among pasta sauces is to take a can of minced clams and pour the juice into at least four tablespoons of butter and olive oil. When this is warmed up, the clams themselves are added, and a full half cup of

Some So-Called Starches

freshly chopped parsley. The sauce is allowed just to come to a boil, and is then ready for use.

The sauce should be well mixed with the pasta. An easy way to do this is to layer it, putting some of the sauce in the serving dish first, followed by some of the pasta, over which more sauce is spooned, and more pasta added, until the whole is well interlarded. It should then be tossed thoroughly with a couple of wooden spoons.

CHEESE IS INDISPENSABLE

Whatever sauce you use, the pasta dish should be served with generous amounts of freshly grated cheese —preferably Romano or Parmesan. This is an absolute must.

If you prefer your pastas in an Anglicized or Americanized form, make a cheese sauce and mix this thoroughly into slightly underdone pasta. Place the mixture in a greased baking dish in a 325° oven. It is well to cover the top with grated cheese, and dot it with butter. This recipe can be varied by the addition of onions, bits of bacon, or anything you happen to care for. We like to add cut-up pieces of thinly sliced baked ham. Leave the dish in the oven till it is browned.

A pasta dish with a salad makes a good buffet meal.

It is easy to prepare, and the contrast of the pasta and the greens is pleasing. Furthermore, the salad furnishes nutritious elements which the pasta lacks.

RISOTTOS

Rice has almost as many uses as have the pastas, but, unfortunately, like the pastas, is starchy, and so should be an object of caution for Americans who, in their middle years, are putting on too much weight. Although rice is of oriental origin it is through the Italians, who brought us the pastas, that we have come to know some of the best rice dishes other than the simple use of boiled rice as a sop for gravy. These are the so-called risottos. They differ from boiled rice in that they are made by first sautéing the rice in olive oil or butter or a combination of the two until it becomes a light golden color. Soup stock or a combination of soup stock and wine is then added, and the whole cooked much as if it were ordinary rice being boiled in water. The proportion of liquid to rice will usually be a little less than in the case of plain boiled rice. Better count on a scant two cups of stock to one of rice, and add more toward the end if needed. Risotto should not be soggy.

Some So-Called Starches

Besides soup stock, various good ingredients go into risottos. Foremost among these are onions, mushrooms, chicken livers and bits of tomato. The Italians make risottos with sausage, herbs and many other odds and ends, including anchovies and other fish. There are almost as many ways of preparing the dish as there are cities in Italy. Italians also commonly use a bit of saffron, both for seasoning and for coloring. Unfortunately, saffron not only is hard to get in the United States but is very costly.

Our own favorite risotto is made by cutting a large onion in small pieces and frying this golden brown in three tablespoons each of butter and olive oil. The rice is added toward the end of this process, so that neither the onion nor the rice shows signs of browning. Soup stock is then added in the proper proportion, and, in the last five minutes, as many chicken livers cut up and sautéed in butter as we have been able to get—say up to a cupful—and an equal amount of cut-up mushrooms also sautéed in butter. The risotto, if served with plenty of grated Romano cheese, is a full meal.

PILAFFS

Close kin to the risottos are the pilaffs, which are usually associated with the Near East. There are various forms of these. A good approximation of one of them can be made by using canned tomato juice instead of soup stock in a recipe which otherwise closely follows the basic recipe for risotto. In parts of the Near East pilaffs are made with wheat instead of rice. As the particular type of grain used for this is hard to find in the United States, few recipes for its use have been worked out.

CURRIES

Rice is an essential accompaniment to a curry. There are at least two main kinds of curries—the so-called creamed curries, which are a European and American development, and the Indian curries, in which the curry powder is cooked with the addition of water or stock. Curry dishes are made with sliced lamb, chicken, shrimp or other shellfish, or eggs, or vegetables. The rice used with a curry can be cooked in any one of the various ways recommended for the boiling of rice. Most of them are described as "sure" or "foolproof." If so, many of us who have tried different ways of cooking rice must be basically foolish. I have never been able to put a pot of rice on the stove with the serene conviction that the finished product would be dry and fluffy—as it should be. On rather rare occasions it has

Some So-Called Starches

turned out like that. But so unsure is it that we have fallen back on the old-fashioned way of using rather more water than is called for, and, when the rice is tasted and found to be done, removing it to a strainer, washing it thoroughly in running hot water and then putting it in a mild oven to dry. This tends to insure a fairly good end product. Most packages of rice have directions on them. I hope you will have better luck in following them than we have had. Incidentally, a final word of recommendation—the brown or unhulled rice is generally regarded as more nourishing than others.

WILD RICE

Occasionally you will find in the markets packages labeled "wild rice." They sell for ten times the cost of domestic rice. This grain is no kin of rice. It grows wild in parts of Wisconsin, Michigan and Minnesota. The Indians in these districts prized it. So did—and do—wild ducks. Duck hunters thus early came to associate wild ducks with wild rice. Many of them insist that the serving of wild rice is a must with wild ducks. It is boiled much as is ordinary rice. Its taste is not unpleasant, but certainly is not sufficiently superior to domestic rice to warrant the excessive price which we are now asked to pay for it. If I were told that never again would I have a chance to eat wild rice, I should bear the deprivation with fortitude, and gladly spend the money that might have gone for wild rice in the purchase of more appetizing and delicious foods.

SALAD **12**

ESSENTIALS

The making and serving of salads is a subject about which opinions differ widely—and strongly. Some would ban all fruits from salads. Others are willing to tolerate a bit of fruit so long as it is not topped with whipped cream and a marshmallow. Californians in restaurants almost invariably begin a meal with a salad. The French usually end a meal with a salad and a bit of cheese. They also serve salad as a vegetable with chicken or lamb. Most Americans, if presented with a salad to accompany chicken or lamb, firmly put it aside and eat it after finishing the meat. In parts of the United States the tightest, hardest heads of lettuce are the most prized, and are quartered and left intact. Elsewhere only loose lettuce is used. Many persons feel so strongly about garlic in salads that waiters in restaurants and clubs often ask if the customer wants his salad "with" or "without."

BASIC SALAD

At the risk of being charged with being didactic I shall start by saying that, at least as the term is used in this volume, the basis of a true salad is fresh lettuce or other uncooked greens, to which may be added portions of uncooked vegetables such as tomatoes, shredded cabbage, raw onions, watercress, celery, radishes and grated carrots or strips of raw carrots. Young spinach leaves are good in salads. So are the leaves of the ordinary nasturtium. Some people add the leaves of wild sorrel.

Whatever the combination of greens, salad is traditionally seasoned with a dressing made of oil—preferably olive oil—and vinegar or lemon juice, with salt and pepper and other condiments to taste. Fish, meat or cooked vegetables in mayonnaise or other dressing are also often served in a salad. There are, besides, mixed salads, often listed in restaurants as "chef's salad" or "chef's special," in which a variety of articles

Salad Essentials

are mixed in with the greens. Strictly speaking, fruits do not belong in true salads, although they are often so used.

When lettuce is used, whether it be iceberg, oak leaf, romaine or whatever kind is in season, the leaves are picked over to remove blemishes, and well washed. They are then drained and dried. We wrap ours in a towel and place them in the refrigerator until needed. When the time comes to mix the salad—which should be as late as possible before serving it—the leaves are torn (not cut) and scattered in the salad bowl. This, incidentally, should preferably be of wood, and rarely if ever washed, being, instead, wiped with a paper towel after using. Such a bowl acquires a patina and flavor of its own.

DRESSING THE SALAD

Experts disagree about the process of dressing a salad. Some insist that the oil must be put on first, and the leaves well tossed in it. Others say that the oil should never be put on first, but, instead, the vinegar and other seasonings. Still others say that the dressing should be mixed in a separate container, and poured over the leaves and the whole then well tossed.

In France, where salads have long been eaten with

avidity, the usual procedure is to start with what the French call a *chapon*, or heel of a loaf of French bread which has been dried and rubbed with a peeled clove of garlic. This is placed in the bowl, followed by the salad greens, which are then covered with oil. Most commonly used in France is olive oil, but there are French epicures who regard walnut oil as preferable. The Abbé Dimnet, whose book, *The Art of Thinking*, published in this country after World War I, set the fashion for a long line of books on self-improvement, always insisted that no salad dressing was fit to eat unless made with clarified butter—and the Abbé loved good food. Whatever oil is used, the leaves are tossed thoroughly with the salad spoon and fork so that each leaf is well coated with oil. Then over the salad is sprinkled a mixture of vinegar and any other seasonings which may be destined for the particular salad of the day. The proportion of vinegar to oil varies from one in three to one in six—usually in the neighborhood of one in four. Such a dressing, be it noted, is far from the acid dressings so often served in American restaurants. The French insist that only high-grade wine vinegars should be used. These may be seasoned with herbs such as tarragon, shallots or basil. When the vinegar has been spread over the leaves they are well tossed again, and are ready to be served. The tradition is that a salad should not stand for more than ten minutes before being served, but we have seen no ill consequences when our salads have had to remain uneaten somewhat longer.

VARIANTS OF FRENCH DRESSINGS

A common and easily made variant of the plain French dressing outlined above is the so-called Roquefort dressing, which is made by taking a tablespoon of Roquefort or blue cheese and mashing this in with the vinegar and other seasonings which are to go into the dressing, and then adding the oil. The whole should be well mixed and poured over the salad greens. Another good variant is to cut up fine, or pound, some fillets of anchovies and mix these thoroughly into a plain French dressing. Frequently persons with fresh herbs on hand chop finely such herbs as tarragon, chives and basil and scatter these over the salad in the process of mixing it. In the making of dressings there can be no rules—only suggestions—as it is a matter of personal likes and dislikes. The same is true of the use of oils other than olive oil. Some find the flavor of olive oil too strong. This is true of some of the heavier oils. We have made it a practice recently to use in equal proportions cold-pressed soybean oil and a good California olive oil. Others prefer to use lemon juice instead of vinegar. This has much to be said for it, provided the lemon is not too bitter. If you are fortunate enough to live where you can get the Meyer lemon, to which reference has already been made, you can make a wonderful dressing with its juice, which is less bitter than are regular store lemons. It has a delicate flavor of its own.

MAYONNAISE

Mayonnaise sauce or dressing is rarely used on salad leaves, but is common as a dressing for cold fish, crab or lobster, or for any one of a number of combinations of items served as part of a salad. Directions for making it will be found on page 48.

SALADS AS MEALS

We have found the salad bowl to be a good medium for the serving of a well-rounded one-dish meal. In addition to the traditional greens we put in anything handy. If there are bits of chicken left over, they are cut up and mayonnaise is added. Sometimes a little fresh tarragon is added to the chicken. If the volume of chicken is scant and celery is available, a half cup or more of diced celery is mixed with the chicken and mayonnaise.

Salad Essentials

If there is cold salmon left, this is made into a fish salad. Occasionally, as indicated in an earlier chapter, we use canned tuna or canned fish flakes with mayonnaise to give more body to a salad dish. Avocados when in season are sliced or halved. We allow at least a half an avocado per person, served without any dressing other than a few drops of lemon juice to prevent discoloring. Excellent meat salads can be made by slicing cold meats very thin and adding crushed anchovies and a variety of herbs to a French dressing in which the meat is marinated and ultimately served. Green beans, of course, are good in a salad. So are canned kidney beans after they are washed thoroughly to remove the juice in which they are canned. They should be mixed with a rather tart French dressing to which some tarragon seasoning powder and fresh cut-up tarragon leaves are added. If we have a mild onion on hand, very thin slices of this are put in with the beans, and the whole turned several times in the course of a couple of hours before being served in the salad bowl.

Potato salad is traditionally a favorite, but often suffers from having too much raw onion in it. This disadvantage is easily overcome by cooking whatever amount of onion you think is appropriate to go with your salad in a small quantity of olive oil until it begins to turn golden brown. This cuts the strong flavor. When cooled it is added to the salad either in the form of a French dressing by mixing into it the proper proportion of vinegar, or by adding the onions to the mayonnaise and mixing both with the cut-up potatoes. Another variant to the use of onions is to mix several teaspoons of chopped chives in the mayonnaise that is to go with the potatoes. We have found that the flavor of a potato salad can be improved by dicing the potatoes raw, and cooking them with a half onion, grated, in a small quantity of soup stock. They are then cooled in a little white wine.

One of the best all-purpose salads is made by mixing into the lettuce a number of different items such as bits of crisp bacon, or cooked ham, and thin slices of cheese, as well as anchovies, and croutons which have been freshly fried in butter, or half butter and olive oil. They should be thoroughly incorporated with the lettuce, so that they will absorb some of the French dressing which goes with this dish. The resulting mixture is both delicious and nourishing.

THE INDISPENSABLE GARLIC

One final word on salad essentials. The French insist —and most gourmets agree with them—that no salad

Salad Essentials

is worthy of the name without at least a hint of garlic in the dressing. By the same token no salad is worthy of the name if garlic has been cut up into it in fine pieces. The use of garlic requires delicacy and tact. But the delicate and tactful use of garlic brings great gustatory delights to all lovers of good food, and, in particular, to those who enjoy good salads.

THE END OF 13
A PERFECT MEAL

Americans love sweets. Yet most Americans past thirty would be less bothered about their waistlines if they cut down on desserts and reduced their over-all sugar intake. Our own routine is to end a meal with fresh or dried fruit or a bite of cheese, usually followed by black coffee. If we have young guests we bring out ice cream which we buy in half-gallon containers and keep in the deep freeze. It is served with homemade preserves and is inevitably welcomed and enjoyed.

THE MERITS OF FRUITS

Skipping dessert simplifies housekeeping and makes it possible to devote more time to the preparation of

The End of a Perfect Meal

more important parts of a meal than sweets. It has the further advantage of being in line with modern nutritional theories. Fresh fruit is, without doubt, an important article of diet. Most Americans eat a fair amount of fresh fruit—or at least did until frozen fruit began to take the place of fresh. Yet fruit is always a pleasant end to a meal, and, thanks to the wide range and variety of fruit production in the United States, it has the merit of offering a variety of choices. Certain fruits, like apples, oranges and bananas, have long seasons which overlap. These fruits are useful in combinations. A favorite in our family is cut-up oranges and bananas, sprinkled with a little sugar. Cut-up apples also go well in this compote.

One of the most satisfactory of the canned fruits is pineapple, which is the better for the addition of a bit of powdered sugar and a dash of rum. Canned pears are improved by substituting a half cup of port wine for the juice in which they are packed, and dusting them with cinnamon.

DRIED FRUITS

Among dried fruits, figs and dates are always good and usually obtainable. In California other dried fruits are also often on sale. Many of them are good uncooked —notably the plumper prunes, and some of the dried apricots. Raisins are still hard to find at their best in this country, despite the fact that they are produced in large quantities. The imported Malaga raisins have a richness which is lacking in practically all American raisins.

THREE POUND-ADDERS

If you feel impelled to serve a sweet, and do not fear for your waistline, try a banana flambé, the recipe for which was brought to us by a friend. Cut in two and slice lengthwise as many bananas as there are persons to be served and sauté them in butter for a minute on each side. Scatter over them a generous amount of brown sugar—say, about a tablespoon per banana. The dark brown sugar is best. As soon as this has begun to melt or caramelize, sprinkle the juice of a fresh lime over the bananas. Then remove the pan from the fire and pour over it a quarter cup of rum. Put a lighted match to it and serve it as it flames. This dish has always met with the greatest enthusiasm—especially on the part of those bent on beginning to bant tomorrow.

Another favorite which the calory-conscious find hard to resist—and which is a sure pound-adder—is good, old-fashioned griddle cakes. We make these not with a ready mix, but by following our own variant of old

The End of a Perfect Meal

stand-bys. To a cup of flour add two tablespoons of sugar, three teaspoons of baking powder, a half teaspoon of salt and a quarter teaspoon of cinnamon. Sift this into a mixing bowl. In the meantime, melt three tablespoons of butter, to which add two-thirds of a cup of slightly warmed half-and-half (the richer the better). In a separate, slightly warmed bowl, beat two eggs. After giving a whirl to the warm butter and half-and-half, add it to the eggs and beat the combined liquid thoroughly. Mix it into the flour and other ingredients until the batter is so thin that it can be beaten easily with the egg beater—about the consistency of store whipping cream. Spoon it onto a hot griddle which has been lightly greased with Crisco, and turn the cakes with a greased spatula after they have begun to bubble. Keep them in a warming plate until all the batter has been cooked. The cakes are served with a choice of honey or maple syrup, or—in those years when our New England friends have had pity on us in our struggle to keep slim and have sent us maple sugar—a mixture of crushed maple sugar and maple syrup. Keep off the scales until you have atoned with a couple of days of low-caloric eating.

The third in this group is perhaps a little less non-reducing than the other two, but has in its favor an engaging name—sillabub. The recipe calls for a pint of sour cream to which is added three-quarters of a cup of dessert sugar (this is even purer than powdered sugar), together with the juice and the grated rinds of three fresh limes. The whole is sealed with a tablespoon of sherry, and is beaten with an eggbeater until it is light and creamy (fifteen to twenty minutes), and then poured into the individual dishes from which it is to be eaten. It should stand in the refrigerator for at least two hours. This is a variant of an ancient English dish which appears to have been a cross between a frothy drink and a dessert. Most recipe books do not even mention it.

Modern housewives whose endless rounds appear to be insupportable should take comfort from the fact that they do not suffer the compulsion of their great-grandmothers to meet the cake needs of their families by hard labor. An old recipe in a notebook of my wife's grandmother, dated 1871, details a fruit cake which starts with the separating of the yolks and whites of fifty eggs, to which are added five pounds each of butter, sugar and flour, together with six pounds of raisins and twelve pounds of currants, as well as citron, ginger, cinnamon, nutmeg and other items in equally formidable proportions. One of the children brought up on this diet is still hale and hearty at the age of ninety—whether because of, or in spite of, I do not know.

IN PRAISE OF CHEESE

In the final analysis there is nothing better than good cheese at the end of a meal. By a "good" cheese I mean a cheese of first quality and distinction—not one of the standardized and basically dull so-called factory-processed cheeses. These mass-production cheeses doubtless serve a nutritional function, but not one of them can compare in distinctiveness and delicacy of flavor with either the originals or American adaptations of such finely flavored cheeses as Camembert, Brie, Cheddar, Roquefort, Edam, Port Salut or any number of other European and locally produced American cheeses.

The kind of cheese which you serve is a matter of personal taste and of what is available in the market. Fully as important as the variety of cheese is what you serve it with. Some of the stronger cheeses of German origin like Limburger and its American descendent, Liederkranz, are usually served with pumpernickel. The better grades of French cheeses, whether made in France or in this country, and the finer Italian cheeses should be served with a French bread or its equivalent, cut in sufficiently large chunks so that there is plenty of crust to be eaten with the cheese. If you do not have French or Italian bread, use crackers of the saltine variety. Due, perhaps, to tradition, a Limburger or a Liederkranz is likely to be served with beer. For the less violent cheeses, however, there is no better accompaniment than a glass of wine. A red or *rosé* wine is preferable to a white.

EAT, BUT DON'T RUN

One of the advantages of ending a meal with cheese is that it is hard to gauge the relative amount of cheese and bread crust which you have on your plate. This tends to make the completion of the meal somewhat of a game, which, in turn, has the merit of counteracting the tendency so common among Americans to feel that they must be on the run the instant they have finished eating. Better a sandwich and a glass of milk enjoyed unhurriedly than to have a larger meal under the compulsion that it is out of the question to sit at the table a few minutes after it is over. American social conventions ban the old Chinese custom of making noises indicative of repletion and satisfaction in the course of, or just after, eating a particularly good meal. Yet even if social discipline demands this sort of repression, it need not imply a denial of the fact of enjoyment of eating. The truth is that a meal is all the better if it is topped off with a cup of strong black coffee, accompanied by pleasant talk. It is well on occasion to follow the evening coffee with a small glass of brandy or other liqueur, as do those masters of gastronomy, the French. This too should be slowly sipped and enjoyed. The French say that it aids digestion. Certainly the French as a race have flourished on the kind of food and drink which has been theirs, except in the years of terrible wars, for upward of two centuries or more.

COFFEE FOR COWBOYS—AND KINGS

A few words about coffee, whether after dinner or at any other time of day. There are wonderful gadgets for making coffee. Some of them are good. Most of them are expensive. We have tried coffee made in many ways, and have found none which is better than the old campcooking method which has stood the test of decades at roundups and on the range. For each cup we allow a heaping tablespoon of regular grind, together with one for the pot. This is put into an open saucepan in cold water, to which is added a pinch of salt. The fire should not be too hot, so that the coffee has time to brew. It is the better for being stirred once or twice. As it approaches the boil, watch it closely and remove it the instant the boiling actually begins. Add a tablespoon of cold water and let it stand a minute, then strain it into a heated container for serving. The method is foolproof—so long as you snatch it off the fire the second it starts to boil. Repeatedly we have been complimented on coffee made this way—and asked the secret. This is it.

WINE AND 14
STRONG DRINK

Wine, if not actually a food, is certainly an aid to good digestion. Furthermore, its consumption is an important part of civilized living. As in other facets of the good life, discrimination, discipline and taste should govern its use. Taken with food, and in moderation, and preferably in company, wine has a mellowing and relaxing influence, and diffuses a glow of friendliness over those who sip it. Furthermore, it enhances the enjoyment of good dishes, and helps to make many rich ones more easily assimilable. This is particularly true of dishes with much butter or fat. Even when wine is added to that simplest of all repasts, bread and cheese, it not only gives a festive touch but brings out the flavor of both. If, in addition, a few olives and figs can be served, the meal will be well balanced as well as good to the taste, as the people of the Mediterranean countries have known for a hundred generations.

THE CLASSIFICATION OF WINES

Wines may be considered under a number of different heads. They may be classified by kinds, such as appetizers, table wines and dessert wines. They may be differentiated by the occasions on which they are served —that is to say, wines for common household use, and those for ceremonial usage, or to be served when guests are to be particularly honored. They may also be classified as heavy or light, dry or sweet, still or sparkling. Most red Burgundies are heavier—that is, richer and more alcoholic—than most clarets from the Bordeaux region. Many Bordeaux white wines are heavier than white Burgundies, or than most German wines. The best-known sparkling wine besides champagne is a sparkling Burgundy. The details of different wines would fill pages.

SHERRY AS AN APPETIZER

The principal wine used as an appetizer is sherry. This is a so-called fortified wine—that is, it undergoes

Wine and Strong Drink

long seasoning, and is strengthened by the addition of brandy. Spain is the home of sherry. It varies from very dry to sweet. The English prefer the sweet kinds. Most Americans like the dry. Incidentally, so do the Spaniards, who, although they drink little sherry, use large quantities of an unfortified wine grown in the sherry district, which is close kin to the wine which serves as the base of sherry. This is called, locally, Manzanilla, and is light, dry and with a delicate flavor. It is consumed with olives, nuts and raisins, usually during the long hours before the Spaniards finally sit down to their evening meal, which is rarely served before 9:30 or 10 P.M. So-called sherries are also made in California, but none of them approximates the Spanish original.

Sherry, incidentally, has plenty of alcohol in it. I have known persons who disapprove of strong drink in general, and of cocktails in particular, to drink sherry with avidity and self-righteousness, convinced that it is as mild as it is delicious. A group of elderly dowagers occasionally foregathered with my mother for a nip of sherry at eleven o'clock in the morning in summer. A favorite topic of conversation was the deplorable drinking habits of their grandchildren's generation. By the end of the second or third round the old ladies were in a glow, all talking at once, ready to put Hitler, or F.D.R., or even Churchill in his place. They would have been outraged had anyone suggested that they had had the alcoholic equivalent of a couple of cocktails.

DESSERT WINES

Chief among the dessert wines are port, Madeira and Marsala. The Hungarian Tokay also belongs in this category. Many of these wines were regarded in Victorian days as excellent for invalids. Whether in fact they are, there can be little doubt that excessive consumption of port and Madeira by members of the British upper classes in the eighteenth and nineteenth centuries was responsible for gout and other illnesses. Most dessert wines are sweet. All of the good ones are expensive. Few of them are particularly digestible. Those made in the United States are often "improved" by the addition of sugars and chemicals which were not in the original grapes.

TABLE WINES

This brings us to table wines. Many books have been written about them, and the tasting and judging of wines has long been an honored profession. I have known groups—I was a member of one for years—to split into factions over the relative merits of Burgundies and clarets. Stories are told of connoisseurs of wines who, by tasting a bottle of wine, can identify the exact location of its production as well as the year of its vintage. Such an accomplishment is rare. Doubtless it brings satisfaction to the possessor and arouses wonder among his friends who lack this sophistication of the taste buds as well as the technological knowledge of the geography of viticulture. This skill hardly seems, however, to rank among the major desiderata of a rich and creative life.

For every one such expert there are hundreds of thousands of Europeans—mostly Latins—who ask of a wine not that it be an absolutely perfect and almost unattainable accompaniment to a meal, but rather that it be a drink which wears well and which is enjoyable for daily consumption. In France they call these wines *vins ordinaires*—that is, plain table wines. Nearly all of them are locally produced, cost little and are usually bought by the barrel and bottled at home. The outstanding characteristic of these wines is that they are made of grapes of the same variety, grown on a comparatively small and restricted acreage. The French and Italians learned long ago not only that the exposure of a vineyard to sun and wind affects the wine produced in that vineyard, but also that the minor differences in soil between a vineyard on one plot and another a few hundred yards away affect the flavor of the resulting wine. As the making of wine is regarded traditionally —and pragmatically—in Europe as a highly individualistic, localized process, the effort is always to strive for such purity as can be attained by using grapes of a particular kind grown in the same kind of soil.

In contrast, many American wine producers have gone in for mass production of wine. They buy grapes of different kinds by the truckloads, and get them from vineyards that are even hundreds of miles apart. The grapes are then processed, many different kinds together, and usually treated artificially so as to give them a standardized flavor. These mass-produced wines are almost invariably inferior. It is amazing that so many Americans have come to enjoy wine when so much that is put out under that name has been marketed by persons interested only in mass sales, who are either consciously or unconsciously ignorant of the elemental fact that wine is a quality product.

GOOD AMERICAN VINEYARDS

Fortunately, despite mass production of cheap and inferior wines in the United States, there are regions in this country in which good wines can be, and are, produced. Among these are parts of California, parts of upstate New York and a small district of Ohio along Lake Erie. Furthermore, within these regions, the owners of good vineyards continue to devote their whole-hearted attention and a large amount of money to the development of really first-class domestic wines. California has a number of such vineyards, notably the Almadén Vineyards, which produce excellent white wines, and one of the best *rosé* wines in the country; Wente Brothers, who produce first-rate wine; the Inglenook Winery, which produces excellent red wines and a fine *rosé* wine; and the Beaulieu Vineyards, which for years have produced rather heavy red wines of the Burgundy and Cabernet type.

IMPORTED WINES

Due to high tariffs most imported wines are expensive. If you like dry white wines, consider some of the German Rhine wines, like the Rieslings and Hochs. The French Moselle wines come from adjacent territory. Some of the best white wine in the world comes from the Burgundy region. Most of the white Bordeaux wines are inclined to be too sweet for more than occasional use. Some of them have fine flavors—this is notably true of a good Château Yquem, or a Château Rabaud—but they do not combine well with many foods. Among the reds there are estate-bottle wines from the Bordeaux region (usually lumped together, in England, under the type-head "claret") and, of course, the famous wines from the Burgundy and Rhone regions. The French are meticulous about the labeling of wines, which means that, as a rule, if a label states that the wine was bottled on the estate and in a particular year, you can rely on this being the case. French wines with general regional labels and no specific designation or date are likely to be inferior.

This is not the place to suggest particular imported wines worth trying. To begin with, most of the good ones are hard to find. In the next place, their enjoyment is in part a matter of taste, in part of experience. The annual production of the finest wines is surprisingly small, which means that they are available only in a few restaurants in France, and are exported in restricted quantities.

THE CARE AND SERVING OF WINES

In the use of wines, it is well again to look to the experience of the Europeans. The French insist that wines should be stored in a cool place. The preferred temperature is in the neighborhood of 50 to 55° Fahrenheit. As it is usually impracticable to maintain a storage room at such a temperature in the United States, the safest rule is to store wines in the coolest closet available. They should never be allowed to freeze. The bottles should be stored lying down, so that the corks do not dry out. When it comes to serving wines, white wine, whether domestic or imported, should be chilled by putting it in the refrigerator an hour or two before the meal. The same is true of a *rosé* wine. Only a champagne should be iced. Red wines are served at room temperature. If you plan to serve a superior imported wine there are two additional preparatory precautions to be taken into consideration. The first is that the bottle should be moved as little and as gently as possible, so as not to stir up the sediment. The second is that it should be uncorked at least an hour before being served. It should be poured with care and restraint to prevent the sediment from getting mixed into the body of the wine. This sort of care is superfluous with young wines.

European custom decrees that white wines should be served with fish, and may be served with chicken. Red wines are usually served with meats, and may be served with chicken or turkey. One of the advantages of a *rosé* wine—the name is given because the color of the wine is about halfway between a red and a white wine—is that it goes well with almost any kind of food.

WINES FOR CELEBRATIONS

Among the wines served on extraordinary—or ceremonial—occasions, the most famous is champagne. It is an acquired taste, and an expensive one. Latin Americans serve champagne lukewarm. North Americans serve it iced. Of all much-praised wines this is the most overestimated and overpriced. For the sum usually paid for a bottle of the imported—that is, the genuine—champagne, you can buy a bottle of some of the very finest wines of the Burgundy or Bordeaux districts—wines which justly can be characterized by the adjective "great." Incidentally, as good champagne cocktails can be made with domestic as with imported champagne. In addition to the customary drops of Angostura bitters, add a tablespoon of cognac or other good brandy to each glass. It improves the flavor and limbers the tongue.

STRONG DRINKS

Strong drinks are welcomed for different purposes. These might be subdivided under the headings: (1) lift; (2) kick; (3) drug; (4) digestive aid.

Wine and Strong Drink

1. There are occasions when persons feel the need of a lift. This is usually due to healthy fatigue, rather than to excesses of either physical or mental expenditures of energy. One of the best ways in which alcohol can furnish such a lift is in the form of some kind of hard liquor, such as Scotch, Bourbon or rum, diluted in a substantial volume of water or soda.

2. If the need is for a kick, many people get it more quickly by drinking cocktails. In the eighteenth century the English and Dutch found that excessive consumption of cheap gin had a disastrous effect on the health of the nation. However costly twentieth-century gin may be in comparison with the gin sold for a few pennies two centuries ago, it would be interesting to learn if scientists have determined whether or not modern gin is deleterious when drunk in substantial quantities. Everyone knows that one man's drink is another man's poison. While I happen to like a very dry martini —we make ours six to one—I am of the opinion that if fewer cocktails were drunk the drinkers would be better off. Certainly they would enjoy their meals more, especially when accompanied by wine.

3. Doubtless the desire of many overworked, overtired persons to drug themselves into a sort of coma so as to forget their problems and troubles is responsible

for the excesses to which the cocktail habit has been pushed. The old Greek adage to which reference has several times been made in these pages—nothing to excess—applies with special pertinence to the consumption of alcoholic beverages. Incidentally, there is no better way of nullifying in advance the enjoyment of a good meal and of good wines than by loading up with too many cocktails. A group of highly experienced gourmets with whom I dined occasionally when I lived in New York made it a rigid rule never to serve cocktails when a particularly great wine like a Richebourg or Romanée Conti, or a very special delicacy like terrapin, was to be a feature of the meal.

4. A word about liqueurs. A good brandy, if sipped slowly at the end of a meal, can be almost medicinal in its aftereffects, as well as agreeable to a satisfied palate. Incidentally, France is not the only country which produces good brandies. We have used for years an excellent Spanish brandy known as "Fundador," made by the old Spanish firm of Pedro Domecq. The Greeks made a good brandy before World War II. So did—and probably do—the Portuguese. If anyone in California makes a brandy comparable to these I have not yet tasted it. In time good brandies should be produced there.

THE SERVING OF LIQUEURS

The pouring of brandy and other liqueurs—there may be a variety to choose from—is usually done by the host. The quantities served are very small. The average liqueur glass holds only a little more than a tablespoon. While "repeats" may be offered, wise drinkers usually are content with one. Even the best of brandies is likely to speed up the heartbeat and may stave off sleep as effectively as coffee.

PLAN **15**

TO PLAN

THREE KINDS OF PLANNING

Over-all planning of meals for several days is not the only—or even the most important—kind of planning. There is also the organization of each meal, including the assembly of the things which you will need for it, and the making of your timing schedule. And there is long-range planning, which has to do with the rearranging of your kitchen so that working in it will be easier and pleasanter. Let us consider this last problem first.

LONG-RANGE PLANNING

If we lived under authoritarian rule one of the most urgent reforms which could be inaugurated would be to make it mandatory for every architect aspiring to plan small houses or apartments to spend at least six months working as cook or kitchen maid. As we live, instead, in the land of the free, architects will probably continue to regard kitchens as unavoidable space consumers, in which a number of standardized equipment units have to be fitted much as are the pieces of a jigsaw puzzle. Thus the architects' customers will continue to be at the mercy of the equipment makers, who have shown rare lack of common sense and ingenuity. The makers of gas ranges for years merely appropriated the shape, size and height of coal ranges, and produced gas-burning stoves that looked like coal ranges. Nine out of ten electric cooking stoves today still are mere adaptations of gas ranges, in appearance as well as in design. Most makers of refrigerators have been content to copy the general dimensions and designs of iceboxes. None of them visualized the absurdity of placing a refrigerator on the floor, which forces the user to bend down dozens of times each day to get things out of it. The makers of storage cabinets have shown no more imagination than architects, having, in fact, taken over from the least imaginative members of that profession the least useful kind of standardized shelving—usually twelve inches deep, and twelve inches between shelves. The resulting waste of space is staggering. Furthermore, the height of counters has been standardized at thirty-six inches above the floor, which means that it is hard to work at them while sitting on even the tallest stool that can be bought in department stores. As a result, housewives spend hours on their feet doing things which could more easily be done while sitting down, and with less expense of energy.

Very probably your reaction to the foregoing is: "My kitchen has all these disadvantages. I hate it. But it would cost a fortune to do it over, and we can't afford it."

Even if this is the case, you might be able to make your kitchen more functional by shifting some of the units. Certainly when the inevitable replacement time comes, you could consider installing more sensible kinds of equipment. At long last a few makers of electric ranges are producing burner units which can be placed wherever you want them—even in a row against the wall, to the horror and indignation of the manufacturers of traditional stoves which project twenty-four to thirty inches into the kitchen. They are even making ovens to be built into the wall at whatever height you like, so that cooks no longer need stoop to baste. Even the refrigerator makers, whose minds so long were stuck in the deep freeze, are beginning to suspect that refrigerator units can be placed horizontally instead of vertically. Give them a few more decades and they will design refrigerators expressly for the convenience of kitchen users.

If at this stage you say: "All right, all right. These may be good ideas for me in the somewhat distant future. But what can I do here and now?" the answer is: Make a detailed study of exactly how you are using your present storage space. Then, list ALL your pots, pans, mixing bowls, spoons, knives and forks and every sort of gadget. Group these under three heads: (1) constantly used; (2) less often used; (3) rarely used. When you have done this, see to what extent, using existing space, you can rearrange your utensils so that the most used will be handy when needed. If your present layout is unsatisfactory, study the possibility of installing movable shelves in existing cabinets, or putting in shallow drawers in place of deep ones, and otherwise making it possible to provide more room for the things most used.

You can do the same with your storage closet, or the shelves where you keep staples, canned goods and other articles of food which do not require refrigeration. The general principles are: (1) Avoid shelves which are more than ten inches in depth as it is hard to get at articles in the back of deeper shelves. (2) Make all shelves movable, so that you may adjust them to the size of the goods to be stored on them. (3) Keep at shoulder height, or slightly lower, all those articles in frequent use, and place those less often used either higher up or nearer the floor. If you have a storage closet or pantry, place nearest the door those articles which you will most frequently need.

Finally, consider the possibility of moving one of your units such as the stove or refrigerator to some place in the kitchen where it will be handier. For this there can be no general rule. When architects realize that even though food comes out of the kitchen, much goes on in the kitchen, they may take a cook's-eye view of the kitchen. This would be a service to humanity. All men—and a good many women—need to become more kitchen-conscious. This includes editors of ladies' magazines who proudly present photographs of kitchens as big as Grand Central Station, filled with equipment that costs as much as a small house, presided over by a damsel dressed by Dior, who obviously maintains her figure by hiking twenty miles a day in her commodious kitchen in line of duty. The best kitchen is compact, with all the essentials within easy reach, and with mileage reduced to a minimum.

Plan To Plan

PLANNING AHEAD

1. Counting Mouths

Wise planning, as already indicated in the chapter on "General Principles," implies not only the provision for the meals that lie ahead but also keeping an eye on cooking today things which can be used in various forms in the next few days. This includes such obvious dishes as roasts and stews. It should also include preparation of generous quantities of vegetables which the family likes in salads, such as potatoes, string beans, asparagus in season, beets and any other favorites. Cold fish is also excellent in salads. Even cold noodles can be used in a salad, as, of course, can cold baked beans.

2. Use Fresh Foods First

If your purchases include fresh fish or fresh vegetables, plan to use them as soon as possible. They deteriorate quickly, and lose their tastiness even before they become inedible. So do the internal organs of animals.

3. Contrasts in Color

Good meals not only should be well balanced as to nutrient values but should present agreeable contrasts in color. There is probably no physiological significance to the old adage that you should not serve a "white" meal. But it is certainly true that if your main dish is, let us say, creamed chicken, and you serve with it rice and cauliflower or turnips, it will be less inviting-looking than if you accompany it with a green vegetable, or beets or carrots. The more attractive the appearance of what you serve, the more it will be relished —provided, of course, it is well cooked and seasoned.

4. *Hot Food Deserves Hot Plates*

This fundamental has already been noted in Chapter I. But it is an essential in good planning. Sometimes it will be hard to manage to heat plates and servers, unless you have a warming oven—which most people lack. However you heat them, it requires forethought to see that the dishes are hot when needed. Lukewarm food loses much of its appeal.

5. *The Mechanics of Serving*

Another detail which the thoughtful planner will consider is how and where the food is to be served. In the good old days everything was put on the table before Father, who piled the plates high and handed them down the table, serving first those furthest away.

Plan To Plan

In many homes Father is still expected to do the carving—if he dares. But in the dim past when there were maids in the land, it was the custom among those who could afford a waitress to have each dish passed to Mother first. If she saw fit, she could wave it away—which she rarely did. Today the problem often arises as to which dishes shall be served by someone at the table, which shall be passed from hand to hand and which shall be brought in by the lady of the house on what she hopes is her last trip to the kitchen for the next five minutes. Each family should settle these details for itself, without benefit of Emily Post, or even of a Vanderbilt (if a Roosevelt may say so!).

6. *Cutting Down Last-Minute Chores*

This is particularly important if you are expecting guests and have no helper in for the occasion. Plan your meal so that as little as possible remains to be done just before or after the guests arrive. If this means omitting a dish of which you are proud, skip it. And don't forget to have a place in the kitchen with a small mirror where a lady can take a last dab at her nose, and put on a final touch of lipstick without being seen. The ideal hostess should be able to look cool as a cucumber even though she has just pulled her head out of the oven.

7. *Changing Menus in Mid-Air*

In every home there come times when unexpected guests show up, hoping to be fed. If the planned meal cannot be stretched, stop it wherever it may be—even if you have a soufflé in the oven—and substitute one of the sure-fire, pretested, all-purpose meals which every good cook should have in the back of her mind. There are excellent pasta dishes which can be made in a short time, and prepared canned goods like corned-beef hash, or roast-beef hash, or codfish cakes, which can be improved by shrewd seasoning, or by the addition of such ingredients as bacon, grated onion, cheese or a bit of fresh tomato. The main thing is to produce a dish with a distinctive flavor. If you are wise, and if the concoction warrants it, do not hesitate to sing its praises as you bring it in. It's good salesmanship—and it puts the guests on a spot.

PLANNING FOR EACH DISH

A time schedule, as we have already indicated, is a great aid in preparing a meal. It helps you do first things first. But you will save effort if you preassemble

Plan To Plan

for each dish the utensils and the seasonings it will require. You can then concentrate on preparing and cooking it without having to search for implements or ingredients. If, for example, you have promised to make pancakes, and you do not use a ready mix, you will want a measuring cup and spoons, a large mixing bowl, and a smaller one if you use beaten eggs, a flour sifter, a large wooden spoon, as well as all your ingredients, including fat for the griddle. The same principle applies in the making of most dishes. A little thought will save a lot of steps.

PREPARATION OFTEN SLOW

Many dishes take much longer to prepare than to cook. Certain recipes call for marinating meats—a process which usually should be started from three to six hours before cooking. Other processes like shelling peas, stringing fresh beans or cutting carrots into strips, take a lot of time. So does the removal of the fibers and membranes of kidneys, sweetbreads and brains. Veal often has to be pounded. No timing schedule can be suggested, as everything depends on the quantity being prepared. You will be lucky if you can shell enough peas or string enough beans for two in twenty minutes. To prepare veal or lamb kidneys for two properly, regardless of the way in which they are to be used, is likely to take half an hour. Wise cooks note the approximate time of preparation of favorite dishes, in addition to the time required for the actual cooking.

ODDS 16
AND ENDS

LEFTOVERS

The use of leftovers has always presented difficulties to writers of cookbooks—and to cooks. Everything depends not only on what, but on how much, is left over.

A few generalities may be helpful. If substantial quantities remain uneaten—such as the remnants of roasts, casserole dishes, vegetables or mashed potatoes—one of the general principles set forth and reaffirmed in the foregoing chapters applies. This is that if the dish is reheated to be used at another meal, the seasoning in it should be changed by the addition of one or more ingredients which the dish initially lacked. If it is to be served cold, a variant of this same principle applies—that it should be accompanied by a distinctive sauce, or incorporated in a salad with a suitable dressing, so that it is presented in a new guise.

If, on the other hand, only small bits remain, they can be incorporated in other dishes. To be specific, a remnant of a sauce can be added to a *roux* and made into an accompaniment for poached eggs, or used as a filling in an omelet. Pasta may be used in a salad, or added to a soup. Rice goes well in soups, pancakes or egg dishes. The remnants of a casserole dish can be put through the blender and incorporated in a soufflé. A bit of soup can be used in a sauce. Small quantities of butter or cheese may be used to enliven an egg dish. No rules or recipes can be given, as everything depends on the particular ingredient remaining.

SUBSTITUTES

When an ingredient called for in a particular recipe is not available, consider possible substitutes. Among the obvious ones are tomato juice, sauce or paste if a recipe calls for solid-pack tomatoes and they are not on hand. So also is the use of cut-up onion tops in place of chives, and of lime, the juice of a sour orange, or a bit of vinegar if a recipe calls for lemon juice and

Odds and Ends

there are no lemons in the house. Cut-up olives can sometimes be used in place of mushrooms, and figs or dates in place of raisins. One of the pastas, or boiled rice or fried hominy, or corn-meal mush can be used in place of potatoes. If no substitute seems to fill the bill, it is possible to try omitting the prescribed article —unless, of course, it is as basic as flour or eggs. The end product will differ from the original recipe, but it may be good.

FOOD FRIENDS

Certain foodstuffs have an affinity for others—or at least for particular seasonings. So, for example, tomato and eggplant go well together. Tomato is the better for the addition of fresh-ground pepper. It also takes kindly to fresh basil and fresh tarragon. Eggplant and garlic make a good combination, as do artichokes and garlic. A genial American of Italian origin, Cademartori by name, who for years ran one of the best restaurants on the Monterey peninsula in California, once described to me the affinity of artichokes and garlic as a "marriage, consummated by olive oil." Cheese and wine complement each other. Wine or brandy added to a sauce or other dish which has a high fat content makes it taste better. It is also easier to digest. Lemon juice or vinegar helps to balance fats. So, also, the combination of foods with different textures can be pleasing. For example, the crispness of uncooked celery is agreeable when celery is added to a dish of creamed chicken. Blanched almonds go well in such dishes. The so-called Chinese peas, which are eaten pods and all, have a crispness of quality which adds a freshness to other dishes, and even to soups—always provided that they are not overcooked. The Chinese have long regarded texture as of great importance in the preparation and serving of foods.

SOME KITCHEN GADGETS

Besides basic articles such as measuring cups and spoons, a chopping bowl, a scale, good-sized salt and flour containers, an egg beater and various sizes of spatulas, we have found a number of kitchen gadgets very useful. Among these are:

A garlic press

A rotary grater

Plenty of mitts to handle hot dishes

A large spoon with holes, to remove and drain articles like poached eggs

A variety of wooden spoons, including at least one with a flat edge

Odds and Ends

    A Pyrex baster
    Metal tongs
    A metal pot grabber
    A soft-boiled-egg opener
    A hard-boiled-egg slicer
    A wire whisk shaped like a spiral spring

Among the more elaborate and costly articles are:
    A Waring Blendor
    An electric knife sharpener
    An electric eggbeater
    An electric coffee grinder
    An electric kettle (This last is equivalent to an extra burner for your stove.)

A PLACE FOR SEASONINGS

A shelf, or series of shelves, not more than two inches deep, within easy reach of the work table where most of the mixing takes place (which, incidentally, should be close to the stove), is also invaluable. Most used among the articles which we keep on this shelf are:

    Salt
    Olive oil
    Vinegar
    Monosodium glutamate

Ginger
Black pepper (in a mill)
Garlic
Basil seasoning powder
Tarragon seasoning powder
Soy sauce
Worcestershire sauce

In addition we have various spices and condiments and some dried herbs.

DEEP FREEZING NOT ETERNAL

So great are the advantages of deep freezing that it is no exaggeration to describe this process as one of the most important developments of our age. As technical devices are improved, the storage period of frozen foods will doubtless increase, and the quality be even better than to date.

While it is difficult to make definite statements as to the length of time which will elapse before frozen foods begin to deteriorate, it is significant that the General Electric Company has printed a booklet for its customers buying deep-freeze units. This includes a table of the approximate storage period of properly packaged frozen foods at 0° Fahrenheit. There are wide differences in the storage time of different arti-

Odds and Ends

cles. Among those listed at less than a month are sliced bacon, sausage (seasoned but not smoked), cooked leftovers, poultry livers, baked cakes, ice cream and chiffon pies.

Among articles good for from two to three months are pink salmon, smoked sausage, cooked shellfish, baked breads and rolls, pies (baked and unbaked).

Articles listed as having an approximate storage period of from three to four months include: bacon (not sliced), cream, most fatty fish, ham, ground pork.

Most other meats are listed as from six to eight months, and most vegetables other than asparagus and stewed tomatoes, from eight to twelve months.

All of which suggests that it is better not to plan on keeping deep-frozen foods for extensive periods. The best over-all advice is contained in the admonition in the G.E. booklet: "Plan to freeze foods to be used from one season to the next." This is a tactful way of saying that frozen foods will not keep forever.

THE CARE AND FEEDING 17
OF GUESTS

Among primitive people guests enjoy a privileged status. Custom prescribes that even known enemies shall be fed, housed, entertained and protected. Certain tribes take it for granted that the host shall lend his wife to a guest—at least for the duration. It is true that the moment a guest steps outside the dwelling his person is no longer sacred. But no matter how eager a host might be to turn out a guest or even to kill him, he would do nothing so long as the guest was within the folds of the family tent. In this connection it is curious to note that the English of the fifteenth century lacked a corresponding solicitude for guests, for it is written of King Richard III, who disliked and suspected one of his advisers, Lord Hastings, that the King interrupted a meeting of the Council Board to announce: "I shall not dine, my lord, until your head is brought to me." Whereupon soldiers hurried Hastings out to instant execution. There is no record of what King Richard ate at the ensuing meal.

GUESTS PRESENT PROBLEMS

In our more compact society guests often present problems. This is true whether they are relatives, friends or strangers; whether they come for cocktails, or for a meal, or to spend the week end, or to settle down for a long stay. However welcome they may be, their presence imposes extra efforts, and custom demands that they shall be accorded special courtesies.

At the risk of trespassing on claims long since staked out by Mrs. Emily Price Post and her imitators, I should like to stress the generality that the shorter the guests' stay, the more important it is to concentrate on their particular likes and dislikes. By the same token it is only proper that long-term guests shall accommodate themselves to the hosts' ways of living.

HINTS ON MECHANICS

Hospitality springs from the head as well as the heart. It is enjoyed much more by hosts and guests alike when the mechanics of entertaining are smooth working. This is as true of a cocktail party and its somewhat insipid relative, a tea, as it is of a meal. Whatever is served, someone other than the host and hostess must see to the passing of drinks and snacks, and to the removal of used glasses and plates. Ideally this is done by a butler or maid. But when these are not present a member of the family, or a friend, may be assigned this chore.

KEEP THEM MOVING

Another equally important task at a large gathering is to see that guests who do not know each other meet, and that guests who find themselves alone or isolated with the same companion for a long time shall be rescued either by asking one of them to come to meet someone else or by bringing up another guest. The purpose is to keep people in circulation, so that they may have a chance to talk to those whom they wish to see. At diplomatic functions it has long been the duty of young secretaries and attachés to perform this shepherding duty. The same end may be achieved in your own house if you can get two or three friends to share in the responsibility of looking after the guests. Their work will be easier if you give them a list of the

The Care and Feeding of Guests

guests. We make it a point to see that these helpful friends are introduced to those whom they do not know. After such parties we have had expressions of appreciation from guests, usually in the form of the statement that never before at a cocktail or tea party had they had a chance to meet and talk with so many different persons.

THE UNAVOIDABLE TIME LAG

A practical word about guests for meals: modern traffic makes it hard for guests to arrive on the dot. Some of the more thoughtful, anxious to be on time, allow so many extra minutes for expected traffic delays that they arrive ahead of the invited hour. Nothing can be so disconcerting to the hosts, who, despite oft-repeated resolutions to be ready at least a quarter hour ahead of time, always have things to do in the last minutes. But as experience teaches that most guests arrive five to twenty-five minutes after the appointed hour, it is well to plan the meal so that there will be ample time not only for traffic delays, but also for the slow drinkers. At the Legation in Budapest the chef and I agreed that meals should be ready to be served a half hour after the time named in the invitations.

THE ROLE OF SNACKS

Before a meal, as at a cocktail party, it is useful to have good snacks to be nibbled with drinks. In the early days in New England the young were told that those who ate the largest helpings of the Indian pudding which was served at the beginning of a meal could have the largest helping of the main course. The lesson deserves to be relearned by their great-grandchildren and other present-day Americans. Cocktail snacks not only act as blotters for strong drinks, but can be important items of a meal—even though the guests may not be aware of it. Professor Charles Townsend Copeland, who was known to nearly sixty years of Harvard undergraduates, would, I am sure, have directed me to add to the above pearl of wisdom one of his favorite comments: *"Verb. sap."*

NOT "WHAT" BUT "HOW"

Some of the writings of the high priestesses of etiquette imply that the fatted calf is none too good for guests. I beg to differ. WHAT is served is less important than HOW it is served. Clearly, the meal should be good, even if it is only a dish of spaghetti. But it is essential that the setting and the atmosphere should exude true hospitality. Some of the most enjoyable parties which we have attended have had simple fare, but it has been served graciously in appropriate dishes, and the guests have been welcomed with obviously sincere warmth, friendliness and spontaneity. Usually these parties have been informal, inasmuch as formality tends to produce social stiffness.

WHO SITS WHERE

Fortunately, most of us who live outside Washington do not have to cope with official etiquette. It is governed by rigid rules of precedence, based on British and continental European, as well as on American, customs. If, for example, persons of equal official rank, such as army or navy officers of the same grade, attend the same function, they take precedence by the dates of their commissions. Two Senators of equal length of service rank in accordance with the date of admission to the Union of their states. But if persons are Cabinet officers of equal rank, they take precedence in the order of the date of the establishment of their departments by acts of Congress. As a youngster in Washington I was given an easy rule to recall this order—to think of St. Wapniac. This saint, needless to say, never existed, but the name represents the departments in the order of their creation—State, Treasury, War, Attorney-General, Post Office, Navy, Interior, Agriculture, Commerce.

In Hungary, among other information which I acquired that had little practical relevance to life in the United States was the fact that Habsburg Court etiquette prescribed that a host expecting royal visitors should meet them at the front door of his house or palace, and should accompany departing royalty to the car. Furthermore, a hostess must place an archduke on her left—not her right—in her own usual place at the head of the table. The host, in like manner, must place a visiting archduchess on his left, and yield to her his customary seat at his end of the table. I also learned that as archdukes and archduchesses outrank everyone except other royalty, protocol decreed that they must sit together if more than one archducal couple was present at the same meal. This may well have helped bolster etiquette, but it is unlikely that it added sprightliness to the conversation.

SILENCE CAN BE GOLDEN

In one respect Europeans seem less custom bound than Americans—they do not feel obliged to talk in

The Care and Feeding of Guests

pairs at every social gathering, without a second's pause. In fact, in France a hostess is expected to know how to guide general conversation, and to enable a guest to be heard who has something interesting to say. This is comparatively easy if the hostess is skilled and alert, for the reason that the French, though great talkers, are also good listeners. At the opposite extreme, many of my Roosevelt cousins, who are as voluble as the French, have long made it a practice, when they get together with their relatives, to talk, all of them at the same time, happily indifferent to the fact that none of them pays the least attention to what the others are saying. An old friend of the family told me that when she was newly married and brought her husband for the first time to a meal at the house of one of the Roosevelts she cautioned him: "Talk as loud as you possibly can, and answer your own questions!"

THE COMPLEAT GUEST ROOM

At the risk of straying too far afield from creative cooking, I should like to say a good word for the author of the precept that all hosts should spend at least one night a year in their own guest room. My wife and I once made a list of things which, at one or other time and place, we had lacked in friends' guest rooms. Here it is:

   Hooks on which to hang clothes in the bathroom and in closets
   Coat hangers
   Water glasses
   Enough pillows
   Extra blankets
   Good reading lights
   Matches
   Ash trays
   Baggage racks
   Note paper
   Sleepable beds

A complete check list would doubtless be even more comprehensive.

HELPING THE HOSTESS

One final word on guests and the serving of guests: the wise hostess, with guests to look after and no servitor or members of the family to turn to, will designate one of the guests to help her in the serving and removing of the dishes, and will ask another to help her in the clearing up at the end of the meal. The guests enjoy it, and are nearly always flattered to be thus chosen. I have known hostesses who disliked to do this, thinking that it was an imposition on the guests. Yet I have seen these same hostesses insist on helping when they are guests in the house of friends, and I have never known guests who were not delighted to lend a hand in any way needed.

"GOOD NIGHT, SWEET PRINCE"

That incomparable word master and social philosopher, Alexander Pope, rendered into English some lines from the fifteenth book of Homer's *Odyssey* which state compactly what we have been trying to drive home:

> True friendship's laws are by this rule exprest—
> Welcome the coming, speed the parting guest.

Yet ever since Homer's time hosts have found it hard to devise a delicate way of suggesting to guests that the end of a perfect day is near. The bluntest instance in recorded literature is the injunction of Lady Macbeth: "Stand not upon the order of your going, but go at once." As midnight has passed and the small hours of the morning have come round, many a modern hostess has probably admired and envied the stark frankness of that determined lady's words. Which is another way of saying that every party, like every chapter, has an end, and that it is better that this end comes too early than too late. As hosts there is little that you can do about it. But as guests you can take your leave at a reasonable hour, with due regard to the time you arrived, and to the time when your hosts —and you—must be up and about on the morrow.

SEX 18
IN THE KITCHEN

Male cooks, except in restaurants, dining cars, steamships, clubs and hotels, have usually been regarded with mixed feelings by the female of the species. Many women, although sure that women are better cooks than men, say publicly that men are better cooks than women. Male skeptics suspect that this is said for ulterior purposes—either to lure a man into the kitchen or to keep him out of it. This much is sure: most husbands in the kitchen use from two to ten times the number of cooking utensils that the orderly preparation of a dish needs, and insist on the uncontested use of every square inch of counter space. Some husbands—and a larger proportion of bachelors—can make creditable dishes, if given time and enough help. Yet not more than one male in fifty deserves being called a really good chef, although the wives of many others encourage their husbands to think that they are wonderful. This can serve two useful ends—it can bolster the male's morale, and, if he is proficient, it can reduce the total number of woman-hours spent in the kitchen for the simple reason that if he does a good job he'll enjoy it, and if he enjoys it, he'll be glad to do it. He'll come into the kitchen without waiting to be asked. The real problem is how to keep a poor cook out of the kitchen. The trials of Job were mild compared to those of the modern woman plagued with a husband who suffers from delusions of culinary grandeur. Such men cannot be checked even if forced to eat their own cooking, and nothing but their own cooking, for a week.

Wives who have struggled through the first part of Simone de Beauvoir's massive book *The Second Sex*—or who are daughters of Eve—know that the proprietary propensity of the average male, as well as his promptness in taking to himself the credit that is due to other members of his family, make a kitchen-welcome husband insufferable when there are guests at the dinner table. He will appropriate all compliments about the food as meant exclusively for himself, even though he may have had no part in its preparation. Good wives bide their time, but even the best can be pushed just so far. There comes a moment when a sense of fairness and a reverence for truth justify a wife in beating the table and crying out: "He didn't have a THING to do with any PART of this meal except to eat it!" This is frankly deflationary. But if the husband is a good cook you won't have many occasions to say it, and if he isn't, he may take the hint and stay out of the kitchen—at least until you send for him at dish-drying time. If he is really skilled, you can boast that you married a *cordon bleu* chef—and remind him how lucky he is that he married a good kitchen maid. Caesar's wife was expected to be above suspicion. But did anyone expect Escoffier's wife to be a good cook?

A POSTSCRIPT ON COOKBOOKS

There are numerous comprehensive, elementary cookbooks. Among these we have found useful the following:

THE BASIC COOK BOOK, by Heseltine and Dow

AMERICA'S COOK BOOK, The Home Institute of the New York *Herald Tribune*

THE BOSTON COOKING-SCHOOL COOK BOOK, by Fannie M. Farmer

Most of the recipes are standard. Anyone using any of these three volumes faithfully and diligently should be able to produce good, plain fare. If you have one you do not need the others.

Three of the more advanced cookbooks, containing excellent recipes, we have found particularly useful:

THE GOURMET COOK BOOK, Gourmet, Inc.
THE GOLD COOK BOOK, by Louis P. de Gouy
THE CORDON BLEU COOK BOOK, by Dione Lucas

One of the books dealing with herb cookery we have found indispensable:

HERBS FOR THE KITCHEN, by Irma Goodrich Mazza
Also good is
THE BOOK OF HERB COOKERY, by Irene B. Hoffman

We have a number of books on cooking with wine. The one which we most frequently refer to is

A WINE LOVER'S COOK BOOK, by Jeanne Owen

On sauces there is much valuable information in

SAUCES, FRENCH & FAMOUS, by Louis Diat

In the realm of professional cooking, or the cooking of highly elaborate dishes, one of the best known is

THE ESCOFFIER COOK BOOK, by A. Escoffier

Many of the recipes in this book require lengthy and elaborate preparations, and call for articles which are difficult to obtain. The author is regarded as one of the great masters of cookery of the last half century. A must for advanced students of cooking, but of only limited value to persons whose time in the kitchen has to be held to a minimum.

INDEX

American Legation, Chef in Budapest, xiii-xiv
Anchovies, as seasoning, 34
Appearances, importance of, 7-8
Architects
    should serve as kitchen maids, 193
    should take cook's-eye view, 196

Banana flambé, 172
Barbecuing, a form of exhibitionism, 122-123
Basil, fresh, uses of, 29
Beans, dried
    baked and Bunker Hill, 149-150
    baked vs. cassoulet, 150
    baked with lamb, 151
    baked, Mexican, how to make, 150
    soy, 151
Blender, use in making vegetable soups, 73
Blot, Mr., century-old culinary authority
    advises against eating ostriches, 100
    advises seasoning buffalo with wood ashes, 120
    extols bear meat, 120
    on bobolinks, 100
    on frogs as breakfast food, 68
    on frog soup, 68
    on how to skin a skunk, 120
    on mayonnaise sauce, 47-48
    on raccoons, 120
    warns against keeping soup in stormy weather, 70

Bobolinks, 100
Bouillon, court, use of in cooking fish, 92
Bowl, salad, 163
Brandy
    after dinner, 191
    as a digestive, 177
    importance of good brandy in seasoning, 35
Broccoli, do not overcook, 141
Broiling, avoid excessive heat when, 11
Brussels sprouts, 141
Buffalo meat, how to cook, 120
Burping, old Chinese custom, 176
Butter, creamed butter sauces, 50-51

Cabbage, how to cook, 15, 140
Cabinets, storage, 193
Cake, fruit, fifty-egg, 174
Calf, fatted, need not be served, 214-215
Canned goods
    rarely really ready to serve, 20
    some musts, 20
Casserole
    chicken, 105
    meat, 130
Casserole dishes, size of, 131
Cassoulet, 150
Cauliflower
    creamed, 39, 140-141
    polonaise, 140-141
Celery, braised, 143-144
Cheese
    as dessert, 175
    as seasoning, 34
    Cheddar, 34
    Parmesan, 34

Cheese—*Continued*
   Romano, 34
   sauce for poached eggs, 55
   should be melted slowly, 18-19
Chervil, uses of, 28
Chickens
   classified by size, 101
   dishes
     baked, 104
     brandied, 38-39
     casserole, 105
     creamed, 109
     grilled over charcoal, 15, 101-102
     leftovers, 109
     roast, 106-107
     how to broil, 103
     how to grill, 102
     sold in pieces, 110
     stock, 110
     stuffing for, 107
     why fried?, 100
Chives, as seasoning, 23
Chores, cutting down last-minute, 199
Chowder
   canned, and wooden nutmegs, 78
   canned tuna, 78
   vegetable, 77
Clams
   minced, 79, 88, 154
   soft-shelled, poached in white sauce, 96
Clam stew, 79
Cocktails, 10, 189-190
Cod, smoked Alaska, 95
Codfish cakes, canned, 88
Coffee, how to make, 177
Color, importance of, 8, 198
Conversation, need not be nonstop, 216-217
Cookbooks, some estimates of, 225-226
Cooking, no short cuts to good cooking, 13
Cooking dishes, as servers, 8, 130-131
Cooks, male, skepticism about, 221
Corn
   baked, 139

Corn—*Continued*
   boiled, 137
   canned, 148
   grilled, 139
   pudding, 138
Counters, kitchen, usually too high, 194
Court-bouillon, use of in cooking fish, 92
Creamed butters, 50-51
Curries, 158

Dates, as dessert, 171
Deep freezing, not eternal, 89, 208-209
Dessert, black coffee as, 177
Desserts, and the waistline, 170, 172
Desserts, types of
   banana flambé, 172
   cheese, 175
   canned fruits, 171
   dried fruits, 171
   fresh fruits, 171
   griddle cakes, 172-173
   sillabub, 174
Diet, importance of variety, 5
Dishes
   cooking, as servers, 8, 130-131
   importance of hot dishes for hot food, 8-9, 198
Don'ts, chapter on, 13 ff.
Drawers, kitchen, should be shallow, 195
Dressing, French
   how made, 164
   proportion of vinegar and oil in, 164
   traditional for greens, 162
   variants of, 165
Ducks, domestic
   fat of, strong, 115
   livers a great delicacy, 115
   prized in China and France, 113
   require constant basting, 115
   soup, how to make, 116
Ducks, wild
   disputes about cooking, 114
   recommendations for cooking, 115

Index

Dyspepsia, caused by fried foods, 17

Eating, enjoyment of, 1
   importance of unhurried, 176
Economizing, false, on seasoning, 9
Eggs
   endless possibilities of, 52
   fried, suggestions for seasoning, 53
   omelets, *see* **Omelets**
   poached
      how to poach, 55
      sauces to accompany, 54-55
   scrambled, how to vary, 53-54
   shirred
      Dutch, 64
      with cream and lemon, 64-65
   soufflés
      cannot wait, 63
      easy to make, 62
      how to make, 62-63
      sweet potato or yam, 146
   eggs static, 65
Entertaining
   mechanics of, 212
   no need for fatted calves, 214
Escoffier, on soaking beans, 149
Escoffier's wife, could she cook?, 223
Excess, nothing to, 14, 21
Experimenting, importance of, 4, 13

Fats, use sparingly, 16
Figs, as dessert, 171
Finnan haddie, 95
Fish and sea food
   early New England
      described by Captain John Smith, 84-85
      described by Francis Higginson, 85
   good brain food, 84
   canned
      clams, minced, 88, 154
      clam stew, 79
      codfish cakes, how to improve, 88

Fish and Sea Food—*Continued*
   Canned—*Continued*
      flakes, useful in salads and other ways, 87
      kippers, 95
      salmon, needs embellishment, 86
      sardines, useful but costly, 86
      tuna, chowder, 78
      tuna, how to use, 86
   cooking
      court-bouillon, use of, 92
      delicate fish best broiled, 91
      fat for frying, 93
      frying, 93
      how to broil, 91
      poached, 92
   fish dishes
      clams, soft-shelled, poached in white sauce, 96
      hash, 87
      sardines, fresh, grilled, 94
      sole, fresh, usually disguised in sauces, 92
   fresh
      lobsters vs. crawfish, 97
      mussels, 96
      shellfish, 96
      trout, 94
      whitefish, excellent but scarce, 94
   frozen, life of, 89
   smoked
      Alaska cod, 95
      finnan haddie, 95
      kippered herring, 95
      salmon, good but expensive, 95
Flavors, avoid mixing strong, 3
Foch, Marshal, counsels audacity, 4
Food, enjoyment of, 1
Food friends, 205
Freshness, importance of, 9, 197
Frogs, for breakfast, 68
Frozen foods, lasting qualities of, 89, 208-209
Fruitcake, fifty-egg, 174
Fruits, fresh, as dessert, 171

Fruits, dried, as dessert, 171
Frying, and dyspepsia, 17

Gadgets, kitchen, list of, 206-207
Garlic
    as a test of cookbooks, 18
    avoid use of in ice cream, 36
    better buy by bulb, 27
    danger of overcooking, 18, 26
    how to cook, 26
    indispensable in salads, 169
    not to be trifled with, 24
    prejudices against, 25
    value of, 25
Garlic press, value of, 25
Garlic sauce, recipe for, 26
Garlic soup, 75
Glace de viande, meat glaze used in sauces, 46
Gravy, mopping up, 2
Griddle cakes, 172-173
Grilled chicken, 15, 101-102
Grilled steaks, 123
Grills for use in fireplace, 103
Guest room, check list for, 217-218
Guests
    allow for late arrivals, 7
    keep them moving, 212
    problems presented by, 211
    speeding the parting, 219
    unexpected, how to feed, 200
    usually late, 213

Habsburgs, seating of, 216
Hastings, Lord, executed before dinner, 211
Heat
    exceptions to low heat, 17
    some hints on, 11
Herbs
    fresh
        some indispensable, 27
        their use and abuse, 27
    dried
        less pervasive than fresh, 30
        uses of, 30
    varieties and uses
        basil, 29
        chervil, 28
        chives, 23
        garlic, see Garlic

Herbs—*Continued*
    marjoram, 28
    oregano, 29
    parsley, 28
    rosemary, 29
    shallots, 23-24
    tarragon, 29
    thyme, 29
Herring, kippered, 95
Higginson, Francis (1587-1630), on New England fish, 85
Hostess
    help for, 218
    should always look cool, 199
Hot dishes, importance of, 8-9, 198
Husbands
    and cooking utensils, 221
    can be useful in the kitchen, 7
    should serve drinks, 7

Imagination, in cooking, 4, 13
Ironware, glazed, makes best pans, 11

Kippered herring, 95
Kitchen
    counters, 194
    drawers, 195
    functional, 194, 195
    planning of, 192-193
    reducing mileage in, 196
    shelves, 195-196
Lamb, shoulder of, grilled, 124
Leftovers, varied uses for, 6, 203-204
Legumes, dried, 148
Lemon juice, as seasoning, 32
Lentils
    soup, 82-83
    with sausage, 151
Liqueurs
    brandies, various makes, 190
    good after meals, 190
    serving of, 191
Liquor, hard
    cocktails and good eating, 10, 189
    uses of, 189
Lobsters vs. crawfish, 97
Lucas, Mrs. Dione, recommends tasting, 12

Index

Macbeth, Lady, and ending party, 219
Males, proprietary propensity of, 222
Marjoram, fresh, uses of, 28
Mayonnaise, 47-48, 166
Meals, should be festive, 8
Meat
  bear, 120
  buffalo, seasoned with wood ashes, 120
  dishes
    casseroles, 130
    grilled shoulder of lamb, 124
    grilled steaks, 123
    meat loaves, suggestions for, 131
    meat salad, 167
  preparation
    barbecuing, 122
    bringing meat to room temperature, 6, 125
    broiling by gas or electricity, 124-125
    grilling over charcoal, 122
    internal organs, 201-202
    pan frying, suggestions for, 127
    roasting, four rules for, 125-126
    stews
      difficult to make, 119-120
      methods of making, 128-129
      seasoning of, 130
  raccoon, 120
  reserves, value of having on hand, 132
  sausages, good ones hard to find, 133
  skunk, how to skin a, 120
  wildcat stew, Chinese recipe for, 121
Menus, changing in mid-air, 200
Mirror, useful in kitchen, 199
Monosodium glutamate, many uses for, 31
Mussels, 96

Noodles, sauces for, 154-155

Omelets
  how to make, 56
  care of special pan, 57
  importance of special pan, 57
  kinds of
    cheese, 60
    French, 57
    herb, 59
    Laurent, 60
    Spanish, 61
Onions
  as seasoning, 23
  baked, 142
  boiled, 142
  French-fried, 141-142
  types of, 142-143
Oregano
  fresh, uses of, 29
  pronunciation of, 29
Ostriches, seldom eaten, 100
Overcooking, evils of, 15-16
Overseasoning, should be avoided, 2-3, 13-14, 21

Pan frying of meat, 127
Pan, omelet, care of, 57
Pans, preferable kinds, 11
Pain killers, used to offset fried foods, 17
Parsley, fresh, uses of, 28
Pastas (macaroni, spaghetti, etc.), 152
  cook just before serving, 153
  do not overcook, 153
  fattening, 152
  how to add sauce, 155
  seasoning
    anchovies, 154
    beef and onion, 154
    cheese, 155
    clams and parsley, 154
    garlic, 154
    tomato, 154
Peas, canned, 148
Pea soup, 73
Pepper, difference between cayenne and paprika, 30
Pilaffs, 157-158
Planning
  three kinds, 192
  kitchen, 193 ff.

Planning—*Continued*
   meals, 192
      cooking today for tomorrow, 197
      importance of contrasts, 197-198
      including leftovers, 6, 203-204
      serving meals hot, 198
Popovers, cannot wait, 7
Post, Mrs. Emily Price, 199, 211
Potatoes
   baked, 145
   boiled, 144
   mashed, with herbs, 3, 145
   seasoning for, 145
Potatoes, sweet, how to prepare, 146
Potato salad, how to make mild, 167
Pottage, Esau's mess of, 82-83
Preparation of meals often slow, 201
Pudding, corn, 138

Raccoons, 120
Ranges, electric, copies of gas, 193
Recipes, not rigid, 3
Refrigerators, unimaginative, 193
Remnants, use of, 6, 203-204
Rice
   curries, 158
   no foolproof way of cooking, 158
   pilaff, a simple way to make, 157
   risottos
      made with fried rice, 156
      seasonings for, 157
Rice, wild, a superfluous luxury, 159
Richard III, decapitated guests, 210
Risotto, 156-157
Roasting
   usually means baking, 125
   four rules for, 125-126
Roosevelt, Theodore
   frying in bacon grease, xiii
   better as President than cook, xiii

Roosevelts, a vociferous tribe, 217
Rosemary, fresh, uses of, 29
Roux, the basis of most sauces, 40

St. Wapniac, 215
Salad
   as a meal, 166-168
   basic, 162
   disagreements about, 161
   garlic in, 168-169
   meat, 167
   potato, 167
Salad bowl, should not be washed, 163
Salad dressing
   French
      how made, 164
      proportion of vinegar and oil in, 164
      traditional for greens, 162
      variants of, 165
   mayonnaise, 47-48, 166
Salmon
   canned, 86
   smoked, 95
Sardines
   canned, 86
   fresh, grilled, 94
Sauces
   discreet use of, 14
   extractive, 38
   four main types, 37
   how to thicken, 46
   importance of, 51
   roux, the basis of most sauces, and how to make, 40
   seasoning of, 45-46
   white
      directions for making, 41
      substitutions for milk in, 42
   varieties of
      béchamel, 43
      cheese, 54
      chicken velouté, 43
      creamed butters, 50-51
      creamed for cauliflower, 39
      creamed tomato, 55
      garlic, recipe for, 26
      ginger mustard, 49-50
      hollandaise, 44
      mayonnaise, 47-48, 166

Index 233

Sauces—*Continued*
  Varieties of—*Continued*
    Mornay, 43
      mousseline, 44
      Point of Whales, 44-45
      poulette, 43
      ravigote, 49
      remoulade, 49
      soubise, 43
      velouté, 43
      vinaigrette, 49
      wine and shallot, 39
Sausages, inferior, 133
Seasoning
  an art, 21
  avoidance of excess, 21
  cautious use of, 2-3, 13-14, 21
  classification of, 22
  importance of experimenting with, 22, 36
  in sauces, 45-46
  list of most-used seasonings, 207-208
  natural seasonings, 22
  the secret of good food, 2
Seasonings, articles used as
  anchovies, 34
  brandy, 35
  cheese, 34
  chives, 23
  garlic
    overcooking, 18, 26
    how to cook, 26
    indispensable in salads, 169
    not to be trifled with, 24
    value of, 25
  lemon juice, 32
  onions, 23
  pepper, 30
  shallots, 23-24
  sherry, 10, 35
  soy sauce, 31
  tomatoes and extracts, 33
  vinegar, 32-33
  wine, 35
Seasonings, bottled, cautions about, 31
Seating, European customs of, 215
Serving meals, mechanics of, 198-199
Sex in the kitchen, 221

Shallots, as seasoning, 23-24
Shelves, kitchen, movable, 195-196
Sherry, importance of good sherry for seasoning, 10, 35
Short cuts, none in cooking, 13
Silence, can be commendable, 216-217
Sillabub, 174
Skunk, Mr. Blot on how to skin, 120
Smith, Captain John, on New England fish, 84-85
Smoked fish
  Alaska cod, 95
  finnan haddie, 95
  kippered herring, 95
  salmon, 95
Snacks, cocktail, utility of, 214
Soda, avoid use of, 147
Solon, Greek lawgiver, advises against excess, 14
Sole, French uses of, 92
Soufflés
  cannot wait, 63
  easy to make, 62
  how to make, 62-63
  sweet potato or yam, 146
Soup
  chicken stock, how to make, 70-71, 110
  chowder
    canned, and wooden nutmegs, 78
    canned tuna, 78
    vegetable, 77
  clam stew (made with canned clams), 79
  cream of fresh tomato, 74
  cream of garlic, 75
  duck, 116
  Esau's pottage, 82-83
  French onion, 74-75
  frozen asparagus, 74
  frozen pea, 73
  frozen spinach, 73
  lentil, 82-83
  lettuce, 76
  stock, how to make, 69
Soups
  as full meals, 82
  canned, how to improve, 80

Soups—*Continued*
    canned, vs. soup stock, 19
    dried, 80-81
    thickening of, 72
    uses of stock, 71
    vegetable, how to make, 72-73
Soybeans, 151
Soy sauce, useful in oriental dishes, 31
Spices, uses of, 30
Squabs, best grilled, 116-117
Steaks, how to grill, 123
Stews
    clam, 79
    meat, 119-120, 128-129, 130
Storage cabinets, usually too large shelves, 193
Stuffing
    for chicken, 107
    for turkey, 111
Substitutes
    examples of, 4-5
    some suggestions for, 204-205
Surroundings, importance of pleasant, 1, 7-8
Sweet potatoes and yams, how to prepare, 146
Sweets and the waistline, 170, 172

Tabasco sauce, use with caution, 31
Tarragon, fresh, uses of, 29
Tasting, importance of, 12
Temperature, room
    in preparing meat, 6, 125
    red wines served at, 187
Thyme, fresh, uses of, 29
Timing, importance of, 6-7
Tomato catsup, leave to lunch counters, 33
Tomato extracts, 33
Tomato paste, cautious use of, 33
Tomatoes
    as seasoning, 33
    broiled, 143
    canned, uses of, 33, 143
Tonics, with alcohol, offset fried foods, 17
Tuna
    chowder, 78
    how to use, 86

Turkey, creamed in pancakes, 112
Turkeys, streamlined, 99, 111

Variety, fundamental in good cooking, 2
Vegetables
    canned, 147
    coarse, 139
    cook in heavy-bottomed pans, 147
    delicate, how to cook, 137
    don't overcook, 15-16, 147
    fresh vs. frozen, 135-136
    legumes, dried, uses of, 148-149
    mild, 143
    seasoning of, 15
    soda, avoid if possible, 147
    types of, 136
    See also under name of vegetable
Vinegar, avoid cheap vinegars for seasoning, 32-33

Water, in cooking, use of, 11
Whitefish, 94
White sauce, 41-42
Wildcat stew, Chinese recipe for, 121
Wine
    as seasoning, 35
    for celebrations, 188
    classification of, 180
    dessert, 182
    foreign, how labeled, 186
    how to serve, 187
    how to store, 186
    importance of, with cheese, 176
    in cooking, 34-35
    in praise of, 179
    mass production spoils, 184
    sherry, 10, 35, 180, 181
    table, 182
    what served with, 187-188
Worcestershire sauce, careful use of, 31

Yams, how to prepare, 146